WHAT REASON DEMANDS

WHAT REASON DEMANDS

Rüdiger Bittner

Translated by Theodore Talbot

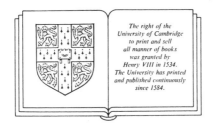

The right of the
University of Cambridge
to print and sell
all manner of books
was granted by
Henry VIII in 1534.
The University has printed
and published continuously
since 1584.

Cambridge University Press

CAMBRIDGE

NEW YORK   NEW ROCHELLE   MELBOURNE   SYDNEY

Published by the Press Syndicate of the University of Cambridge
The Pitt Building, Trumpington Street, Cambridge CB2 1RP
32 East 57th Street, New York, NY 10022, USA
10 Stamford Road, Oakleigh, Melbourne 3166, Australia

© Verlag Karl Alber GmbH 1983
English translation © Cambridge University Press 1989

Originally published in German as *Moralisches Gebot oder Autonomie*
by Verlag Karl Alber GmbH 1983
English translation first published as *What Reason Demands* by
Cambridge University Press 1989

Printed in the United States of America

Library of Congress Cataloging-in-Publication Data
Bittner, Rüdiger, 1945–
What reason demands.
Translation of: Moralisches Gebot oder Autonomie.
Bibliography: p.
Includes indexes.
1. Ethics.   I. Title.
BJ1114.B5713   1989   170   88–20340

British Library Cataloguing in Publication Data
Bittner, Rüdiger
What reason demands.
1. Ethics. Reasoning
I. Title   II. Moralisches Gebot oder
Autonomie. *English*
170

ISBN 0 521 35215 0 hard covers
ISBN 0 521 37710 2 paperback

Contents

Preface

The aim of this book is to get clear about morality. In the form of a story, it would tell of someone who sets out to justify or in some other way understand the moral demands often confronting him. Many tries at justification fail. But at last – and here is the point of his story – he finds in the attempted justification through autonomy a cogent argument for there being no valid moral demands after all. He then embarks on a new journey, intending to find out what rational action looks like under the condition of autonomy and in the absence of moral demands. With this new beginning the story ends.

More precisely, the book proceeds as follows: The first chapter introduces and explains the question 'Why should I be moral?' (Sections 1–19) and then considers various responses (20–27). Pursuing one objection, the chapter concludes by developing a new question: 'Should I be moral?', in the sense of 'Are moral demands valid?' (28–32). The second chapter examines responses to this question based on certain essential attributes or accomplishments of human beings, namely, their rationality (35–41) and sociability (42–46). The third chapter examines responses appealing to contractual relations between human beings (47–64). The fourth chapter considers whether the validity of moral demands can be based on promises and develops a theory of promising (65–84). The proposals for justification reviewed in the first four chapters all fail. The fifth chapter turns to Kant's thoughts on autonomy. It begins with an account of what 'autonomy' means (86–87); in particular, it clarifies a confusion, heavy with consequence, underlying Kant's use of the word (88–93). It then examines those arguments by Kant for the validity of moral demands that do not fall back on the autonomy principle, and it finds them unsuccessful (94–101). Arguments for the autonomy principle are next taken up – first that offered by Kant (102–107) and then one of my own, based, however, on Kant's analysis of action (108–118). Finally, the consequences of the autonomy principle for moral philosophy are drawn. The principle indeed enables one to state a plausible concept of moral laws, as well as a way to prove their validity (122–123). But it precludes valid moral demands (124–127); and moral laws, even if sometimes valid, have no practical import (128). The sixth chapter asks what the good reasons for actions are (129–133). The answer: A good reason is one that fits into the agent's plans and experiences in a way that makes sense (137). To use the traditional term, a good reason is a prudential reason (150–151). I then explain this answer (138–139), with particular reference to the philosophical tradition on prudence (151–161), and defend it against a series of objections (162–174). The last of these objections I take up in the seventh chapter. There I examine Hegel's arguments for not tolerating the contingency of prudential reasons (181–192) and for passing beyond the standpoint of finitude, where prudence is moored (193–203). But these arguments do not stand scrutiny.

The present book is the English translation of a work that appeared in 1983 in German under the title *Moralisches Gebot oder Autonomie*. That book, in turn, was the revision of a manuscript with which I habilitated in 1982 at the Freie Universität Berlin. The present English edition revises and expands the German text in many places. The substance of the argument has not been changed, however. The division into chapters and sections also corresponds to that of the original.

The ideas presented here have been with me for quite some time now. So I am grateful to the many people whose conversation and criticism often helped my thinking along: Barbara Leucht, to begin with; Hans-Georg

Gadamer, who encouraged reflections, forming the core of the present work, that I brought forward in his colloquium around 1970; above all, Jens Kulenkampff, with whom I discussed practically every point of this book at the time of its first writing; Dieter Henrich and Reiner Wiehl, who critically read the first version; Margherita von Brentano, Günter Patzig, Ursula Wolf, and especially Ernst Tugendhat, who incisively critiqued a later version; and many others, with whom I discussed these ideas in various connections. I am grateful to Raymond Geuss and to an anonymous reader for the Cambridge University Press for good advice on preparing this English edition, and to Theodore Talbot for the translation itself.

Hildesheim, Germany   RÜDIGER BITTNER

I. Why should I be moral?

1. 'Learning to live through philosophy.' Philosophy seeks to know how the world is constituted as a whole and how one is to live there.
2. Moral philosophy seeks to clarify the meaning of morality in view of its importance in our lives.
3. The question 'Why should I be moral?' introduced by an example.
4. The interest of the philosophical question 'Why should I be moral?'
5. Objection: Taking moral demands as the starting point distorts our view of morality. Response to the objection.
6. Starting from moral demands avoids ontological problems.
7. In the case of moral demands, unlike that of moral judgments, the claim made on action is clear.
8. Academic discussion of the question 'Why should I be moral?' has distinguished several senses it may have. In fact, the question is univocal.
9. The question does not ask for the motives of moral action.
10. The question does not ask for considerations of self-interest that would speak for moral action.
11. The question does not ask for considerations of general utility that would speak for the existence of a moral society.
12. The question does not ask for considerations that show the importance of moral laws.
13. The question does not refer to any particular moral problem. The distinction between internal and external moral questions does not help.
14. The question asks for a justification of the general demand to act morally.
15. Explanation of 'justify a demand'.
16. One asks for the grounds of a demand in order to find out if there are grounds for acting according to the demand.

1. Education requires philosophy. We learn to find our way about in the world, and in learning this we help others as well. We learn this in many sorts of ways, and thereby help in many sorts of ways. But to learn our way thoroughly, or to help others reliably, we have to know how the world as a whole is constituted and how one is to live there at all. Philosophy is the attempt to inform rationally about this. It redeems itself if its answers to such questions about the world and one's life in it satisfy educators, those being educated, and those educating themselves. In the Platonic tradition, the idea of learning to die through philosophy has become a powerful one.[1] But "the true need for philosophy is directed toward nothing else than learning from and through philosophy how to live."[2]

2. In societies such as ours, education includes, as an important part, moral education. We are guided and guide others toward actions, convictions, and ways of living preferred or distinguished according to moral principles. For many people this is the chief task of education. But even those who demur, who perhaps find moral education as such misguided, have themselves been morally educated in one way or another and have encountered moral demands and judgments made with the claim to direct their behavior. In this way, morality differs from religion. Compared with the situation a few centuries ago, many people today have no religious upbringing in any significant sense. Although morality may someday come to the same end, at present it still reaches all of us. Given its extensive and profound influence, we may well wonder: Exactly what moral principles do we use to evaluate actions and character, how are these principles related to other considerations we allow to guide our actions, and what are the grounds on which the demands connected with moral principles are based? These and similar questions are, according to the preceding criteria, philosophical, and hence questions for moral philosophy. Demanded is a clarification of what morality means for life.

3. As an example of moral education, consider admonishing a child to leave the last remaining piece of candy for his momentarily absent brother, rather than eat it along with his own portion. Neglecting what would be a good or poor means of effective admonishment, we may suppose the child to ask in return why he should not eat the last piece if he really wants to. Many sorts of responses come to mind, but three typically stand out. First: "Your brother would also like to eat a piece of candy, and you rob him of this pleasure by eating the last piece yourself." But the child could easily counter: "That's fine with me!" Second: "In the future, your brother will likewise refuse to share; so you are only hurting yourself by not leaving him a piece." "But," the child can reply, "he doesn't need to find out that there was anything to share in the first place." Finally: "Eating the last piece behind his back is just unfair, and thus wrong, morally bad." But to this the child can reply: "Still, why shouldn't I? Even if it is morally bad, I still would like to know why this is a good reason for me not to do it. Why should I be moral at all?" An answer to this question is the aim of what follows.

4. It might be objected that the foregoing is a construction, not an example: Only philosophers, not children, ask such questions. But on the one hand, this is not so clear, because children often do ask questions that, when rephrased, turn out to be philosophical questions. On the other hand, even if it is true that children do not actually ask this question, the question is not therefore pointless, for someone could internally carry on the argument just described whenever he admonishes in this way. Every educator has had the unpleasant experience of strongly supporting an action only to realize that it could just as well have been left undone. The wrong fortresses are often defended with too much ado. Experience might teach us to reconsider whether we really should urge the child to leave the piece of candy for his brother. We would take many different things into account, but one consideration would be especially important: Why shouldn't the child, after all, eat the piece himself? This internal dialogue can then proceed as the external dialogue sketched earlier. The objection that this consideration is again philosophical is trivial, judging from what was said in earlier sections (1,2). The examples of external and internal dialogues simply show that reasoning is not unnatural by virtue of being philosophical. The examples suggest points at which it would be appropriate, or at least intelligible, to pursue such considerations and thus situations in which answers would be desirable, as well as those in which answers might affect behavior.

5. It might be further objected that taking moral demands as the point of departure distorts our perspective on morality. Morality, it might be said, does not consist in a bunch of demands made on the unwilling. Morality, by nature, can be understood only as what, before the making of any demands, people already are in their institutionally ordered associations. Morality is a matter of something like custom, not of demands: shared ways of life, learned by example and imitation. In contemporary German philosophy, this approach has been especially advanced by Hans-Georg Gadamer and Joachim Ritter,[3] both of whom refer to Aristotle and Hegel for support. Among recent American philosophers, Michael Sandel and Michael Walzer presented similar conceptions.[4] But this view of the matter is unsatisfactory. What we need to know is whether what people are in their institutionally ordered associations is good and rational. True, this question would be dismissed as misguided by those who hold that the objective relations between human beings determine what is good, bad, or permissible.[5] In fact, this conception is itself refuted by the very emergence of such questions. No shared way of life enjoys a degree of trust among those concerned that would warrant presuming that they take morality itself to be simply defined by that way of life. No institution has been able either to avoid or to overcome permanently all doubt and criticism. The mere fact of radical social critique, not an evident absurdity, prevents one from identifying morality with any given order of association.[6] Another question arises: How can moral education enable one to present moral demands tellingly and make them more effective? Education certainly does proceed by example and imitation, not primarily by raising demands. But this sort of mediation does not entail that what is mediated can be grasped only as a shared way of life. After all, moral teachers who prefer examples to demands will encounter the same challenging response: Why be moral and follow the examples?

6. Moral demands also deserve preference over moral

norms or principles as the starting point for our discussion. Although we can speak of justification, validity, rationality, and so on, both with respect to moral demands and with respect to moral norms or principles, moral demands, in contrast to moral norms and principles, do not pose any ontological problems. Moral demands exist in the same innocuous sense of 'exist' in which greetings and insults can also be said to exist. Moral demands are simply one kind of thing that people utter. But it is not easy to see in what sense and under what conditions it can be said that a moral norm or principle exists.[7] This is not to say that in any given case we can easily determine whether or not what is uttered is a moral demand. I claim only that once this matter is decided, talk of the existence of moral demands will create no further problems.

7. True, this holds for any sort of moral utterance, so that as far as this argument goes, we could as easily have begun with, say, moral judgments as with moral demands. Actually, however, moral demands are still preferable as a point of departure, for the claim that moral demands make on our acting is clear. Such a claim is not so striking in the case of moral judgments, simply because they are judgments. Our attention must be drawn to it, for example, by being told that such a claim is logically connected with moral judgments[8] or that moral judgments usually are made with the purpose of making such a claim on acting.[9] Moral judgments would be the appropriate starting point if morality were something that people *are* in institutionally ordered ways of living together (5). Moral judgments would then express what Hegel graphically called the "masses of the ethical substance."[10] Because things are not that way, because morality is not how people are constituted but what they are required to do, moral demands recommend themselves as our starting point.

8. The question 'Why should I be moral?' has been widely discussed among contemporary academic philosophers.[11] They have tried to sort out the different meanings that the question so worded can have and to give the corresponding answers. One such answer will be that the question under a given interpretation is meaningless. But actually the question is not ambiguous. The words may indeed in different contexts mean different things or be differently understood, but this is true for every expression. The question has a natural context, namely, that of such examples as we have just seen, and for this context a natural sense. In the following, I shall determine this sense more precisely, at first negatively, by eliminating what the question does not mean (9–13), and then positively (14).

9. The question 'Why should I be moral?' has often been understood as demanding a motive for moral action.[12] The concept of a motive is itself extremely unclear, despite extensive discussion[13] that I cannot take up here. A rough sketch of what we ordinarily understand by 'motive' will have to do. Two notions may be distinguished. On the one hand, we call a 'motive' what is referred to in sentences of the form 'He acted out of . . .' by whatever expression fills in the blank.[14] On the other hand, a motive is, to use Aristotle's expression, the "whence the movement" of an action, its psychic source of energy, what Kant graphically called its *Triebfeder* (incentive).[15] However the two notions may relate to each other, whether they be contradictory, compatible, or even equivalent, for the present it matters only whether or not either of them can be used to explicate the question 'Why should I be moral?' Immediately we see that this is not possible for the second, for then the question would mean 'From what motive, that is, driven by what force, should I act morally?' – which does not even make sense. One cannot speak of an obligation to act from this or that motive, if 'motive' means a spring of action. Drives and forces operate or fail to operate according to their nature and independently of any acts of will that could be brought under an 'ought.' If the question instead means 'What force in fact drives me to act morally?', then it does make good sense, but a sense quite unlike that originally intended. The question is now theoretical; it concerns the drive mechanisms for particular actions, and this information is at best indirectly relevant for future action – unlike the earlier question. But the same applies to the first sense of 'motive.' A person can act from jealousy, revenge, boredom, or pure pleasure, and accordingly these are motives. But to ask 'From what motive should I act?' in this sense of 'motive' is again meaningless, because one has no say in the matter. On the other hand, the question 'From what motive of this kind do I actually act when I morally act?' does make sense (even if it is not likely to find a unique answer), but it is a theoretical question and thus differs from the earlier one. In this study I shall not consider motives any further.

10. The question 'Why should I be moral?' also does not ask for considerations of long-term utility, which could make doing what we are morally commanded to do seem to lie in our own interests.[16] We may indeed be able to imagine situations in which the question is intended this way. It is more plausible to assume, however, that whoever does ask in this way is aware that some actions are morally commanded that may run counter to self-interest entirely. Anyone who knows this will not ask the question, not because it would be meaningless but because it would be superfluous. One already knows that no consideration of long-term utility could in principle justify the moral claim. The question, then, does not ask for the justification of moral claims in terms of personal utility. Rather, that the search for such a justification must fail is what gives the question its point. The questioner might explain himself as follows: "Concerning my long-term interests, I am happy to receive advice, for I know how easily people are mistaken about them. But a demand that, as we know, in principle does not rest on considerations of my long-term interests, and may at best happen to coincide with them, must somehow establish its claim. I am not asking what interest I could have in renouncing an interest that belongs to my considered overall interest. Clearly, such an interest does not exist.[17] But I should like to learn on what, if not my interest, the demand can be based."

11. Another possible meaning of the question was thought to be this: 'What considerations of general utility speak for the existence of morality as a social institution?'[18] To be sure, 'institution' probably is not the appropriate term. What is meant, namely, our actions and speech as oriented by moral ideas, as having reference to them or as understandable only with respect to them, does not exhibit the self-reliance and internal coherence expected of institutions.[19] Probably we should do better to speak of a practice of morality that is widespread in our society. All the same, the question did not concern the general utility of this practice. The question was not 'Why should *one* be moral?' in the sense of 'Why is it good that morality is being practiced in our society?' but 'Why should *I* be moral?' The first question answered, one may still wonder about the second and not thereby show failure to understand what was already said. The two questions are different.[20] Their difference does not prevent us from trying to answer the second question on the basis of an answer to the first, that is, to answer the question 'Why should I be moral?' by appealing to the general utility of morality. But additional argument is needed here. Mere reference to the general utility of morality is not by itself a sufficient answer to the question 'Why should I be moral?' It is not self-evident that one should be moral just because the general use of morality benefits all.[21]

12. Henrich understands the question 'Why should I be moral?' to be about the importance of moral laws.[22] What he means by 'importance' is best seen from the way Henrich, interpreting Kant, answers this question:

> It is important for me to accept moral laws, because only through them can I combine the implications of my life's natural orientation, originally constituted by the ineluctable ideas of reason, with the equally ineluctable certainty that I should bind my action to principles of reason, into a unified conception of myself, of my position in two worlds and of the origins and determination of my knowledge.

It is natural to think that the need for an integrated form of life is a particular case of the interest one generally has in one's own well-being and to think, accordingly, that the question about the importance of moral laws is a special instance of the question about the utility of moral action (10). But Henrich rejects this approach. On the other hand, the question of the importance of moral laws is to be "sharply distinguished from the question of their validity." We need not go into whether or not these conditions allow us to give a tenable notion of the question about importance. It seems clear that ordinarily, as in the situation described in (3), the question 'Why should I be moral?' would be understood as a question not about the importance but indeed about the validity of moral laws. An unsatisfactory answer, so the idea goes, would allow the questioner not only to make light of moral laws that he continues to recognize as valid but also to regard them as void entirely.

13. The particular moral demand made on the speaker that led him to ask 'Why should I be moral?' is also irrelevant to that question. The speaker has asked not 'Why should I do this thing?' but 'Why should I do anything that is morally demanded of me?'[23] Here it might seem plausible to follow Carnap[24] and distinguish the latter question as an external, and the former as an internal question.[25] But in this way we can easily forget that questions about particular demands naturally lead to the question about moral demands in general (3,4). Moreover, Carnap's account does not explain how in any given case we come to know the framework relative to which we can sort out questions as internal or external. If we ourselves stipulate this framework, then the distinction becomes tautological, and those questions will be external that we have chosen to call such. If we instead discover this framework, then it remains to be said how and where it can be discovered. It is advisable, therefore, not to grant special status to the question 'Why should I be moral?' Regardless of whether or not it is raised on another level than are questions about particular moral demands, we need only say that it is a different question.

14. Contrary to what this variety of possible meanings may suggest (9–13), 'Why should I be moral?' leaves little room for misunderstanding. Getting back to example (3): A demand is made and, on being challenged, is justified with the remark that it is a moral demand. But this remark justifies only under the presupposition of another demand, namely, the general demand to act morally; for if the remark would only classify the demand under some group or other of demands, such as, say, 'annoying' ones or those 'typically coming from parents,' it would not justify the demand. The remark must be understood as subsuming the demand under a group for which a general demand is supposed to be already in force. This general demand to act morally, or to be moral, will be questioned in turn regarding its grounds. I am told that I should be moral. Why, actually? And so the question is 'Why should I be moral?'

15. We are seeking grounds for the general demand to act morally. We are looking for a justification of moral demands as such.[26] But this explanation of the question 'Why should I be moral?' may itself seem to need explaining. For one thing, a general explanation of 'ground' may be demanded, whether it be a question of grounds for statements, demands, or whatever else can be given grounds. I shall not attempt such an explanation, but assume that talk about grounds is in general sufficiently clear. On the other hand, one might take special issue with this talk of justifying a demand. We know, one might say, what it means to justify a statement, but not what it means to justify a demand. But in fact it is clear what it means to justify a demand. It means to bring forth considerations showing that the demanded action is worthy of recommendation. It means to show what is good in the action, that by virtue of which it recommends itself. The question 'Why should I be moral?' thus asks, in effect, 'What is good about moral action?' One might object that our inquiry then runs in a circle: Not much is gained if we justify moral demands by means of still other moral judgments, namely, judgments of the sort that a certain type of action is good or recommendable. But actually these are not moral judgments, and 'good' and 'recommendable' here do not mean 'good in moral respects' and 'recommendable for moral reasons.' But neither do these predicates signify that the actions in question are useful to the person addressed and that they are recommendable as a means for realizing other aims of his. Otherwise, in our quest for a justification of moral demands we would have unreasonably committed ourselves to accepting as a justification only the reduction of moral demands to considerations of general utility.[27] But what it means to say that morally demanded actions are good is not fixed in this way. 'Good' does not mean 'morally good', 'aesthetically good', 'useful', or the like. Rather, 'good' always means, put simply, that something is preferable – for whatever reason.[28] Asking what is good about morally demanded actions, one leaves open under what perspective or on what grounds these actions will prove to be good. One is demanding not some particular sort of grounds but any grounds speaking for moral actions. What sort of grounds these are remains to be seen.[29]

16. The justification of a demand shows what is good about the action demanded. This lets us understand why a person might seek a justification, although justification might be thought superfluous (i.e., inconsequential) because the demand, once made, calls for the action, whether or not the demand is justified. But to the person on whom the demand is made it does make a difference whether a justification is given or not. She must choose between heeding and not heeding, and for this choice a justification of the demand weighs heavily. This is so because the grounds for a demand are grounds for a corresponding action as well, for to show that an action is recommendable is to give reasons for so acting.

17. The proposed account of 'justifying a demand' can be countered by the example of extortion. One person demands a certain action of another and promises either great harm if the action is not done or great reward if it is. Here the first person seems to have advanced a consideration showing that compliance with the demand is recommendable. Yet we would not say that she has thereby justified the demand. But that is because the action demanded is recommendable only by virtue of the promised harm or reward. This condition rests in the hands of the one making the demand, however; this person has herself made the action recommendable, rather than shown it to be recommendable independent of her doing. Hence, the promise of reward or harm does not count as advancing, in the sense intended here, a consideration showing that the action demanded is recommendable. We need not attach a corresponding clause to our explication of 'justifying a demand,' however, because this case is irrelevant to the justification of moral demands. That the stated circumstance is the reason for our not saying that under such conditions the demand has been justified becomes clear once we alter the situation. It may turn out that it is not the person demanding the action who brings about the promised harm or reward, but these will follow omission or performance of the action without her doing, by natural necessity. In this case we do call the notice of impending harm or reward a justification for the demand.

18. From what has been said, justifying a demand is not distinct from justifying advice. After all, advice, too, is justified by indicating in what way the action recommends itself. Indeed, we are saying the same thing when we make a demand and when we give advice, namely, that a person ought to do something. We just say it in different ways, depending on our relationship to the person. The tone in which we say it varies in the two cases. Yet this difference does not mean that advice and demands require different sorts of justification.

19. We can formulate what it means to justify a demand or advice by means of the corresponding double meanings of 'require' and 'advise.' Someone commands an action, 'requires' it – a demand is made. One justifies the demand by showing that the action is indeed 'required' or 'called for' – required in the sense in which something can be required without anyone having required it. Likewise, we justify advice as to a course of action by showing that the person in question will be well advised to act this way – in the sense in which one can be well advised without actually having received advice.

20. Among the responses to the question 'Why should I be moral?' put forward in the literature (8), that of Kurt Baier is perhaps the most natural and has been given the most attention. Baier follows Hobbes and concludes that if all or at least most people always or usually act morally, then all will live better than they would if actions were not usually moral. It is therefore in the interest of each person that action always, or at least usually, be moral. "It is therefore also in your interest," so the argument might be turned against our challenger, "and that is the reason why you should be moral."[30] A similar argument, but more precise and detailed than that of Baier, is given by Neil Cooper. In order to avoid the unwelcome effects of inadequate cooperation, we are advised at least to appear altruistic to some extent. So that others can be sure of our own cooperation, and will thereby be induced to cooperate themselves, however, we are also advised actually to internalize the rules of moderate altruism.[31]

21. This is the argument from the utility of the general acceptance of morality. It breaks down at the point already noted (11): We do not see why, for this reason, one really should be moral oneself. Granted, for the moment, that it lies in the interest of each of us that generally, that is, by and large, people act morally, it does not follow that it lies in the interest of each of us that he or she for his or her part act morally. It will often happen that a person will prefer that state of affairs in which all except that person will act morally.[32] Nor do we need actually to adopt altruism for ourselves in order to assure others of our cooperation. To appear altruistic suffices, and it is less costly.[33] Hence, self-interest alone does not give a reason for actually being moral. But the interest that others have in the condition of general morality, and hence, among other things, in my acting morally, will give me a reason to do what is desired of me only if I have already adopted the rule of complying with their interests even at the expense of my own. But such a rule will hardly be adopted except for moral reasons. But whether or not these will be good reasons is just the question. The general interest in general morality, then, does not provide an answer.[34] The use of Hobbes's idea to justify a legal order that prevails by forceful means is another matter. We need not decide the cogency of such an argument here. Yet it draws support from just that circumstance in which the moral version of the idea breaks down. The persistent discrepancy between general and individual interests may make it seem advisable to entrust the safeguarding of a social order lying in the general interest not to individual actions but to public force.[35] However that may be, clearly such an argument for the existence of a legal order fitted with coercive powers does not by itself provide us with grounds for acknowledging a corresponding rule as obligatory for our own actions, for one can consistently employ oneself for the establishment of a certain social order through public force and yet not consider this order binding for oneself, and indeed go as far as possible to exempt oneself from it in one's own interest.

22. Recently, Baier modified his answer to our question, conceding that the interest each person has in general morality does not yet give sufficient reason for one to act according to moral principles. Two further conditions must be met. First, the society must generally acknowledge moral demands as ultimately decisive in the determination of action. Second, these demands must be just, and they are just if, compared with other social orders, they can be said to serve the interests of all people most nearly equally. If these conditions are satisfied, then each individual has the strongest of those grounds for acknowledging moral demands that could be grounds for every individual. Hence, each person has sufficient grounds for accepting moral demands.[36] But again the conclusion does not follow, even if the premises are granted. Moral demands that are just may provide each person with the best of those grounds for accepting the demands she shares with everyone else. This is not to say that each person has the best grounds for accepting them, simpliciter. Just as before, one will prefer that situation in which all but oneself acknowledge these just demands. To insist, on the contrary, that no such private grounds, but only grounds shared with everyone else, may be considered is to appeal to a moral demand whose validity we must first justify.

23. A second response to the question 'Why should I be moral?' has been most clearly made by Philippa Foot in her 1958 article "Moral Beliefs."[37] To be sure, she does not treat the question 'Why should I be moral?' but only 'Why should I be just?' But this is no restriction. We can easily proceed to a corresponding thesis about morality in general if Foot's principles provide a satisfactory response in the special case of justice, for she contests the very opposition in principle between self-interest and morality that I have assumed (10). Following Plato and Aristotle, she claims that acting justly lies in one's own interest in the long run and is morally demanded for just this reason. Those who desire a situation in which everyone except oneself acts morally (21) deceive themselves about their real interests. Only the just are happy. Foot argues her claim by noting the discomforts, troubles, and losses that unjust action brings on even those who manage to avoid the threatened punishment. If we add up all of the various costs of vigilance, lack of trust in one's neighbors, psychological hardening, and so on, then the unjust life strikes a negative balance.

24. Against Foot, it can first of all be objected that her balance of costs overestimates the morality of how the world goes. As things are, it is troublesome to be just, not to be unjust.[38] To be sure, we have to be vigilant now and then not to be caught doing things that are punishable or otherwise sanctioned. But usually an easy, because long-practiced, dissemblance suffices, not to mention the great number of ordinary, unremarkable acts of injustice. On the other hand, Foot certainly underestimates the demands of morality. True, a just action that currently is burdensome may well prove salutary in the long run. But sometimes it does not, no matter how long one waits. Sometimes one is harmed by one's justice.[39] Yet the action is still morally demanded even in these cases. Hence, moral demands cannot be justified by considering what is useful to oneself.[40] Foot concedes that now and then injustice brings us further, and she gives the example of someone who would rather suffer death than do an injustice. But the example refutes her thesis. If justice led someone to ruin and he nevertheless had good reason to act justly, as Foot says,[41] then her claim is false that moral reasons recommend only actions that are in the interest of the agent. A critic of current moral demands may indeed contest their claim to override all considerations of utility. But to justify these demands by reason of self-interest is impossible. Foot, by the way, later corrected herself on this point (171,172).[42]

25. That justice serves one's own good can be defended in another way, though probably not a way intended by Foot. One could declare that the overall good and evil that the just person experiences in the world are immaterial compared to the happiness created by the internal harmony he or she owes to virtue. Such a view guided the British sentimentalists, who followed ideas of stoical ethics. I shall not pursue this line of reasoning here, not because it is clearly mistaken but because its discussion would require a detailed notion of what is meant by the happiness of a well-ordered mind, relative to which whatever else is called happiness or unhappiness vanishes. Explication of this notion would require a study of its own.

26. As direct answers to the question 'Why should I be moral?', answers specifying reasons for acting morally, we have only these two from Baier and Foot, who for their part follow the classical proposals of ancient and modern philosophy. In contrast, most earlier writers who treated the question 'Why be moral?' believed the question meaningless.[43] One reason they often gave was that any answer would prove tautological, being a justification for acting morally that itself is moral.[44] Yet, as noted earlier (15), it is not true that the justification must itself be moral (i.e., rest on moral principles). What we are looking for is any justification for heeding moral demands, not necessarily one that itself is already moral. Bradley objected to the question 'Why be moral?' from the other direction: The question already presupposes that moral action is acceptable only as a means to something else and so fails to do justice to what morality really means.[45] Brock has formulated the two objections with the following dilemma.[46] The grounds we are seeking for moral demands will themselves be either moral or extra-moral. Justification by means of moral grounds will not do, for their validity is precisely the issue. But moral demands cannot be justified on extra-moral grounds either; for as moral demands, they claim ultimate authority in the determination of action. If their validity is based on extra-moral considerations, such as those of self-

interest, then their claim to authority extends only as far as
these extra-moral considerations support this claim. Hence,
not moral reasons but, rather, extra-moral reasons ultimately are decisive in the determination of action. So extra-
moral reasons do not justify moral demands. Hence, it is
impossible to justify them, and the question of their justification is meaningless.

27. By 'ultimately decisive' I mean what is usually expressed by saying that moral demands are 'overriding' or
'final.' The idea is this: If there are two reasons or two
demands for actions that cannot both be satisfied, and only
one of the two is a moral reason or demand, then it maintains the claim to determine action, and the other loses this
claim. Taking legal parlance as our model,[47] we can say
that moral demands take precedence over all other claims
on acting. But 'overridingness,' so defined, determines the
resolution only in cases of conflict between moral demands and other kinds of demands. Precedence can be
taken only in cases of conflicting claims. That the justification of moral demands with extra-moral reasons robs
them of their overriding power, as the argument claims,
thus presupposes that these extra-moral reasons sometimes conflict with the moral demands.[48] Of moral demands that never come into conflict with extra-moral considerations we can well say that whenever they do come
into conflict with extra-moral reasons, they retain the up-
per hand; in other words, they are overriding. But a suc-
cessful justification of moral demands by means of extra-
moral reasons immediately rules out any conflict with the
latter. Anyone who justifies a demand gives reasons for
accepting it to the extent of its applicability (16). Reasons
that suggest acting counter to the demand under some
conditions are not reasons that can support this demand.
Basing morality on, say, self-interest involves showing
that, appearances to the contrary, no conflict between
them is possible. If their conflict does remain a possibility,
the alleged justification of morality does not obtain (21).
So it is false that justifying moral demands by extra-moral
reasons robs them of their claim to override in the determination of action. If it did rob them of this claim, no

justification would have been given in the first place.[49] The error may rest on a confusion. On the one hand, we often do give moral reasons alongside other reasons for the same action. We then misleadingly say that moral reasons are supported by the other reasons, which is only to say that they all point in the same direction. This does not preclude that under other circumstances the two sorts of reasons may speak for opposed ways of acting. On the other hand, sometimes one sort of reason is justified by, and reduced to, another sort of reason. In this case, the one sort of reason can no longer conflict with the other. We must therefore distinguish between parallel and serially conjoined reasons, and the present case concerns the latter.

28. None of the answers to the question 'Why should I be moral?' has been convincingly argued. Moral demands have not been justified, nor has the question of justification been shown to be out of place. So it seems that moral demands might admit of, but in fact do not receive, justification. But we usually reject as void claims that, though justifiable, are not justified. The implication for moral demands seems to be this: Because unjustified, they should be considered invalid.

29. But precisely this inference from 'unjustified' to 'invalid' is being questioned in the case of moral demands. Regardless of whether or not we treat other claims this way, moral demands are said to be beyond justification; that is, they are valid independent of whether or not they receive justification. Several writers have expressed this view.[50] In a sense, they too give an answer to the question 'Why should I be moral?', but only a tautological answer: because it is right.[51] In answering this way, they intend not to give up the validity of moral demands but to reinforce it. Sometimes this idea is even presented as a part of the moral point of view, so that inquiry after reasons for moral demands becomes itself morally questionable.[52] Even if we set aside this move, we still will be precipitous in discarding moral demands on grounds of their unjustifiability so long as we do not consider the possibility of their being valid independent of justification.

30. There is, however, a presumption in holding that

moral demands are valid independent of justification.
Standing before the piece of candy, the child had asked
why he should heed any moral demand such as the demand to leave the piece for his brother (3). We now reply
to him that there is no answer to his question, and we
cannot show him why it is recommendable to heed moral
demands (15); yet we claim that it may still be true that he
ought to heed moral demands. To say that a moral demand is valid is to say that it can rightly be said of the one
on whom the demand is made that he ought to follow it;
that is, it makes a justified claim on his acting. Then we are
using the word 'valid' in a different sense than the ordinary
sense, in which those rules are valid for a particular group
of people that are 'in force,' that is, roughly, that are such
that people more or less reliably follow them or that people are more or less reliably sanctioned in cases of non-
compliance – a sense of 'valid' that will not be used here.
Now, to sever the validity, in the sense indicated earlier,
from the justification of moral demands is a presumption,
for the following reason: Anyone who heeds a moral demand and knows its justification does what he ought to
do, but also knows why it is good that he does it. Anyone
who heeds a valid moral demand while *not* knowing its
justification, however, does what he ought to but does not
know what is good about acting that way, other than that
the action fulfills a just demand. In a way, he is acting
blindly; for he does know what is demanded of him, and
does it, but he does not know any justification of why it is
demanded of him. He may, indeed, have good grounds
for his action; for if he knows that a moral demand made
on him is valid, then he already has a good reason for
heeding it. But whoever knows not just this but also why
he ought to do something has another sort of reason for
acting this way. The presumption lies in asking a person to
be content sometimes with reasons of the first kind.

31. The presumption can be countered in various ways.
On the one hand, it may be rejected as really intolerable.
There simply are, one could argue, only good reasons of
the second kind for action, reasons also telling us what is

good about the action in question. That it satisfies a valid moral demand is never alone a good reason for an action. The idea that moral demands are valid independent of justification is simply vacuous; one does not know what such an unmediated 'ought' could be.[53] Whoever thinks this way makes the verdict on the validity of moral demands depend entirely on the answer to the question 'Why should I be moral?' Because no satisfactory answer is to be found, he will regard moral demands as empty. On the other hand, one can deny that a presumption is involved. The idea that someone simply ought to do something, without knowing why, causes, in this view of the matter, no difficulty. An unmediated 'ought' may exist; it just may be a fact that some action is required. Anyone who thinks so will regard the answer to the question 'Why should I be moral?' as irrelevant to the verdict on the validity of demands. It is not obvious which of the two sides is right; it is even difficult to recognize what sort of arguments could be given in the dispute. We shall do well to leave the question open and proceed from the assumption that rules out less – that of the second position – according to which moral demands can be valid independent of justification, and an unsatisfactory answer to the question 'Why should I be moral?' does not suffice to decide against their validity. This assumption does not suffice to decide in favor of their validity either. Even if there is no justification of moral demands in the sense of 'justify a demand' given earlier (15), and moral demands may nevertheless be valid (29), it still must be demonstrated with reasons that they are really valid![54] Under this assumption, the question 'Why should I be moral?' turns out to be insignificant, but in its stead we have the question 'Should I be moral?', which is to say, 'Are moral demands valid?' This is a different question. Earlier we asked for a justification of moral demands; now we are seeking reasons for the claim that moral demands are valid. These, we have seen, are reasons of a different kind. Whoever knows the justification of a demand knows why he ought to heed it, but whoever knows the reasons for asserting its validity knows only that he ought to heed it (30). In the following, we shall take up reasons that have been given for claiming that moral demands are valid.

32. The difference between justifying a demand and demonstrating its validity can be made clear by an example. Automobile owners are obligated to present their vehicles at regular intervals for safety inspection. A person might ask the reason for this demand: "Why must I have an inspection every two years?" The rule will be justified on the grounds that it guarantees a certain measure of safety of vehicles involved in traffic and thereby decreases the danger to life and limb. But the person may also demand proof of the regulation's validity: "Must I have an inspection every two years?" As an answer, he will be referred to the regulations governing vehicle registration. The example does not mean that the validity of moral demands should be understood in the same way as the validity of the demand to present vehicles for regular inspection. But the difference between the questions of why a moral demand is valid and whether it is valid or not is the same as that between why one must present one's vehicle for inspection and whether or not one must do this. Joseph Raz distinguishes in the same way between content-dependent and content-independent justifications of a command. The former indicates that the performance of the demanded action is desirable, the latter that the command was given by some authority having jurisdiction in the matter and is valid.[55] Common to justifying a demand and demonstrating its validity, however, is that in both cases one gives reasons for an action that fits the demand. Whoever realizes why she ought to do something knows grounds for doing it (16), but so does anyone who realizes *that* she ought to do it. Hence, one seeks proof for the validity of a demand for the same reason one seeks a justification of the demand: in order to learn the reasons for heeding it.

II. Should I be moral?

       among others must acknowledge in certain cases universal
       practical judgments also to be reasons for action.
46. Criticism of the argument: The idea of oneself as a person
       among others implies only that practical judgments ex-
       tended from one's own case to other cases be regarded as
       meaningful, not as valid. Nagel's argument, moreover,
       does not allow any substantial moral consequences to be
       drawn.

33. The arguments for the validity of moral demands I
next consider are in a certain sense all arguments ad hominem. What they try to show is not that moral demands are
valid but that certain essential attributes or accomplishments of human beings make it impossible for them not to
regard moral demands as valid – not to 'acknowledge'
them, as I shall also say in the following. If someone pro-
fesses not to regard moral demands as valid and yet makes
a claim on the attributes and functions defining human life,
then he is either deceived or insincere, or he does not know
what he is saying. Now actually we may disregard the
difference between showing that moral demands are valid
and showing that they must be considered valid. For the
realization that given certain basic features of our lives we
cannot help but acknowledge moral demands is tantamount to having their validity demonstrated to us.[56] In the
following, I shall examine arguments of this kind only
concerning whether or not the acknowledgment of moral
demands is necessarily bound up with these attributes and
functions. I shall not examine the claim that these attributes and accomplishments *are* essential to human
beings. They are, in at least a historical sense: They belong
to the traditional idea of the human essence.

34. The arguments fall into two groups. One group is
based on human rationality. They try to show that either
rational communication in general, rational communication of certain kinds, or the mere competence to communicate rationally entails the acknowledgment of moral demands. The other group proceeds from human sociability.
They aim at showing that actions or agents, being understandable only in social terms, must be understood as sub-

ject to moral demands. The two groups of arguments thus correspond to the classical, in particular Aristotelian, dual notion of human beings as both rational and political beings.[57]

35. To begin with the arguments from rationality: In his 1970 article "Must One Play the Moral Language Game?" Alan Gewirth tries to show that someone who judges on the basis of utility what is best to do is rationally bound to accept moral judgments and so to acknowledge the corresponding obligations. True, Gewirth does not give reasons for the last step, from accepting moral judgments to acknowledging moral demands, although this step is clearly problematic. Perhaps he would appeal to Hare on this point.[58] Be this as it may, the argument for the necessity of accepting moral judgments runs as follows: If someone (1) wants something, (2) believes that a certain action is a necessary and sufficient means for obtaining what he wants, (3) believes that he has a choice between this action and others and that this action requires some effort on his part, (4) believes that he is capable of performing it, and (5) believes further that nothing stronger speaks against performing the action, then he also (6) believes that he ought to perform the action. The entire statement – if (1)–(5), then (6) – is analytic. But from the particular judgment he makes according to (6), that he ought to perform the action, there logically follows a universal judgment: Whoever wants the thing referred to in (1) ought to perform the action. But this universal judgment is already a moral one. It meets Frankena's four conditions on moral judgments: Whoever adopts the judgment regards it as a prescription for action, concedes to it universal validity, and regards it as overriding in the determination of action; and the judgment recommends actions or omissions because of how the interests of others will be affected.[59] Whoever meets conditions (1)–(5), therefore, must also accept a moral judgment.

36. The argument is questionable at several points – for instance, whether the inference from (1)–(5) to (6) is analytic, or whether the universal judgment obtained really does meet Frankena's last two conditions. But I am con-

cerned only with the transition from the particular judgment (I ought to perform the action) to the universal judgment: Everyone who wants the thing mentioned in (1)
ought to act this way. The inference is not convincing.
What is rightly said of me, that I ought to do a certain
action, for example, must not for this reason be assertable
of everyone. True, Gewirth's universal judgment refers
not to everyone in general but only to everyone who
wants the thing mentioned in (1). But this restriction does
not suffice to make the universal judgment follow from
the particular one. If someone does want this thing but,
unlike me, does not have the power to obtain it, then we
may not say of him that he ought to do the action in
question, whereas this may very well be said of me. A
universal judgment having some chance of following from
the particular one would then be this: Everyone for whom
conditions (1)–(5) hold ought to do the action. Gewirth
claims that this judgment follows from the particular judgment because the latter rests on the satisfaction of conditions (1)–(5). Not only is it true that I, for whom conditions (1)–(5) hold, ought to do the action; from this
statement the universal judgment obviously does not follow. Rather, it is true that I ought to do the action because
these conditions hold for me, that is, because I want this
thing, because I see in the action a necessary and sufficient
means, and so on. But if I ought to do the action *because* I
meet the conditions, then everyone meeting them ought to
do it. What is a reason in my case must be a reason in every
other person's case as well. But actually it is not true that I
ought to do the action because conditions (1)–(5) hold for
me. Gewirth's claim that this is the case evidently rests on
his other claim that the statement – if (1)–(5), then (6) – is
analytic. But even if this claim is correct, (1)–(5) entail not
that I ought to do the action but only (6): I believe that I
ought to do the action. That someone satisfies the series of
conditions (i.e., wants a certain thing, finds she has the
necessary and sufficient means, etc.) at most allows us to
infer that she believes she ought to perform the stated
action. But this says nothing about whether she really
ought to do it. If then the claim 'I ought to do the action

because the conditions hold for me' is not true, we do not have grounds for inferring the universal from the particular judgment.

37. The argument can be corrected. Suppose that someone meets conditions (1)–(5) and therefore, in accordance with (6), believes that he ought to do the stated action. Now he may say that he ought to do the action because (1) he wants the thing mentioned, (2') the action is necessary and sufficient for obtaining this thing, (3') he has a choice between this and other actions, and this action requires effort on his part, (4') he is capable of performing it, and (5') nothing further speaks against doing it. Then, (1) and (2')–(5') would be grounds for belief (6). On the other hand, (1)–(5) are grounds – according to Gewirth, logically sufficient grounds – for claiming that such a belief exists, that is, for claiming that (6) holds. But the agent's statement that he ought to do the action because conditions (1) and (2')–(5') hold in his case seems to entail that anyone for whom they hold also ought to do the action, and so we would obtain the universal judgment. But in the first place, this result would be considerably weaker than the one Gewirth desires. The acceptability of a moral judgment cannot be demonstrated to anyone who believes only that he ought to do the action, a belief he must have if he has a will and beliefs as described in (1)–(5). At best, it can be demonstrated to someone who believes that because (1) and (2')–(5') hold for him, he ought to do the action – someone, that is, who ventures to justify his beliefs about what he ought to do. But in the second place, even his statement does not entail the universal judgment. If someone believes that he ought to do a certain action, then a plausible thing for him to do is to give reasons like those adduced in (1) and (2')–(5'). But from (1) and (2')–(5') it does not logically follow that he ought to do the action. Statements together justifying another statement need not for that reason logically imply the statement. Someone who has properly described another's situation by means of statements like (1) and (2')–(5') may rightly object to the imputation that he has thereby implicitly judged what the other person ought to do. Someone, then, who justifies his belief about what he ought to do by pointing out that certain conditions hold has not thereby accepted the universal judgment that everyone ought to do this under these conditions.[60]

38. In his 1978 book *Reason and Morality,* Gewirth offers a new argument for the validity of moral demands. The argument functions like the earlier one: It is supposed to show that someone who allegedly considers her actions only from the prudential point of view cannot avoid acknowledging moral demands, if she is not to contradict herself. The argument basically runs as follows: Anyone who in acting pursues certain goals, which she therefore considers goods, must also consider to be goods the necessary conditions of her pursuing any goals in acting; she therefore considers her freedom and well-being goods, even essential goods. But anyone who considers freedom and well-being essential goods believes that she has a right to freedom and well-being. But anyone who claims such a right for herself must, because she bases this claim solely on her attribute of being an agent, acknowledge the same right for all agents. Hence, she cannot avoid accepting as valid the demand to act in accordance with this right of everyone to freedom and well-being. But this demand is the supreme principle of morality.[61]

39. This argument improves on the earlier one by not attempting, on the basis of Frankena's criteria, to characterize general rules of prudence as moral judgments. We now have an obviously moral principle that supposedly anyone aiming at some goal in his actions is required to acknowledge. Yet the obvious moral character of this principle also allows us to spot easily the weak point of the present argument. It is located in the second of the three claims, namely, that anyone who considers freedom and well-being necessary goods believes that he possesses a right to freedom and well-being. Whoever considers freedom and well-being necessary goods may demand of others that they not interfere with his freedom or well-being, and assuming that these are necessary conditions of his actions, he has the best grounds for making this demand. But a demand for which one has good grounds is not therefore a justified demand, namely, if we say that those demands are justified which demand what one is entitled to have. Gewirth does not overlook the fact that it is part of the concept of having a right to something that the thing be due to one. But he fails to show that a person is due, or believes that she is due, whatever she needs even essentially.[62] The argument's third claim runs aground with the second. That all have a right to freedom and well-being was to be required on the grounds that claiming this right for oneself rests on ascribing attributes to oneself that all goal-conscious agents must ascribe to themselves. But because the second claim of the argument is false, claiming such rights for oneself actually does not rest on ascribing to oneself attributes everyone ascribes to oneself. Finally, even the first claim does not pass scrutiny. Whoever considers something a good does not therefore also consider a good whatever is a necessary condition for obtaining that thing. According to Gewirth's way of talking about goods,[63] something is a good for someone if that person's actions are aimed at obtaining it. But often the necessary conditions for achieving a goal are not such that actions will in turn be aimed at them. Often these conditions are simply given. And whether or not in some other situation in which they are not given we will make an effort to bring them about is not yet decided by our using them to reach some goal in the present situation in which they are given. So I do not see on what grounds the necessary conditions for achieving some goal should themselves be called goods.

40. The so-called transcendental arguments of moral philosophy aim at showing that acknowledgment of moral demands is necessarily linked to entry into either rational communication in general or rational communication of a particular kind.[64] Thus, A. Phillips Griffiths claims for some moral demands that their acknowledgment is essential to the possibility of moral discourse.[65] This thesis is stronger than Hare's thesis, which earlier we used to supplement Gewirth's argument (35). For Hare, evaluative use of certain moral terms involved acknowledgment of the corresponding moral demands,[66] whereas now entry into a moral discourse, of whatever kind it may be and whatever concepts it may use, presupposes acknowledgment of certain moral demands. According to Hare, refusal to acknowledge certain moral demands excludes a person from using the corresponding moral terms, or at least from using them evaluatively. For Griffiths, on the other hand, whoever refuses acknowledgment is barred from all moral discussion. Some German authors have made even stronger claims. According to the Erlangen School[67] and K. O. Apel,[68] participation in rational communication in general, not just moral discourse, involves acknowledgment of a principle of rationality on which the justification of moral demands ultimately can be based. Finally, in Habermas's view, not only those who do communicate rationally but also all who can speak and act are committed to acknowledging this principle of rationality.[69]

41. But all these claims – that moral discourse, or rational communication, or the competence for rational communication presuppose the acknowledgment of principles of rationality – are obscure in their talk of 'presupposition.' The authors use different terms to describe the relation. Griffiths uses 'presuppose,' Habermas speaks of an 'implicit acknowledgment,' and occasionally one speaks of participants in rational communication 'having always already accepted' a principle of rationality or, to use Kambartel's metaphor, 'already standing on the ground of this principle.' Two ideas are being offered here: On the one hand, 'implicit acknowledgment' suggests a relation of logical implication. Whoever takes part in rational communication, in this view, acknowledges principles of rationality, because the latter follow from the former. On the other hand, if the person has 'always already acknowledged' principles of rationality, one seems to have in mind states or events such that the one never arises without the other. The term 'presupposition' is neutral, being used for both kinds of cases.[70] Concerning the first interpretation, upholding a relation of logical implication, it simply is not true that the concept of rational communication includes the idea of an acknowledgment of principles of rationality; it does not include the idea in an obvious way, as the concept of blue obviously includes that of being colored. In Kant's phrase, the insight that rational communication is always tied to such an acknowledgment would extend, not explain, our knowledge.[71] Nor does the one include the other in a nonobvious way, as, for example, mathematical statements include others without it being obvious that they do. In mathematics, we expect a proof to reveal the implication that is not visible at first sight. But no one has given an argument, akin to mathematical proof, revealing the implication nonobviously holding between rational communication and the acknowledgment of principles of rationality. Hence, if 'implicit acknowledgment' is to mean 'implied acknowledgment,' there is no such thing. Regarding the second interpretation assuming two events or states such that the one never occurs without the other: Experience runs counter to the thesis that rational communication occurs only among people who acknowledge certain principles of rationality; for one can talk rationally with any person, except the severely mentally handicapped, about some things sometimes. Not only those who regard certain principles as valid, but all people, are rational – in the weak sense of sometimes being amenable to rational communication. Now, on the one hand, one might reply that I have not refuted the thesis that rational communication occurs only with the acknowledgment of principles of rationality. We need only assume, the reply would go, that as all people are rational, so all people acknowledge principles of rationality. But this assumption seems false, for some people say that they do not acknowledge these principles. To be sure, they may be lying or deceived. Yet the evidence for this diagnosis is not apparent. It cannot be based on evidence that these people continue to participate in rational communication despite their declared nonacknowledgment of rationality principles. They do continue, but using this as evidence for their actually acknowledging rationality principles makes a tautology of the thesis that rational communication rests on this acknowledgment. On the other hand, it could be replied that the acknowledgment of rationality principles is not a constant attitude of a person but is a state in which that person sometimes is and at other times is not. So it may indeed be true, the reply goes, that everyone can at some time be spoken with rationally; this is because everyone, at least some of the time, regards rationality principles as valid. But sometimes rational discourse miscarries, and in some of these cases it is because the participants do not acknowledge certain rationality principles. But this construal of the thesis robs it of its import for a theory of morality; for if in not acknowledging rationality principles a person does exclude herself from all rational communication, then we can with some plausibility say of her that she cannot avoid acknowledging principles of rationality. As matters now stand, she can easily avoid this: In particular cases she takes back her acknowledgment of principles of rationality, and nothing more happens to her than that rational communication does not occur in just these cases – which probably is just what she intended. It is not difficult, then, to avoid regarding rationality principles as valid. Hence, there can be no question of proving the validity of moral demands in this way. To sum up the argument: The claim that rational communication presupposes acknowledgment of principles of rationality cannot be understood as a claim of logical implication; no such thing has been proved, nor is it obvious. Nor can it be understood as claiming that the one never obtains without the other, for rationality principles are not acknowledged by all people at all times; some people refuse to do so. But if they are acknowledged by only some people at all times, then the claim that rational communication does not occur without the acknowledgment of rationality principles is false, for with anyone we can sometimes speak rationally. But if they are acknowledged by some or all people only sometimes, then the claim may be true, but it is too weak for the purpose of the argument, for then there is no reason to assume that the principles of rationality really are valid, not just sometimes believed to be valid.[72]

42. The second group of arguments for the validity of moral demands, arguments from the sociability of people, includes that given by Richard Norman in his book *Reasons for Actions*. There he transfers Wittgenstein's private-language argument to moral philosophy.[73] Like the language a person uses, what she wills and does not have meanings that only she can understand. Willing and acting become intelligible only through a system of concepts shared by the members of a society on which they can come to an understanding.[74] This system necessarily includes normative and, in particular, moral concepts. Actions can therefore be understood only in terms of the moral concepts of the given society, and any action resisting classification under these concepts must be regarded as irrational. Neither critique nor justification can reach behind the moral claims designated by these concepts. Critique cannot, for though a given norm can be questioned or set out of action, this can be done only by appeal to other socially given norms.[75] Justification cannot, for though a given norm may be made plausible, this can be done only by describing the place it assumes in the given system of moral concepts or concepts of action in general, not by giving any independent reasons.[76] The system as a whole cannot be attacked or defended.[77] Our actions thus invariably fall under moral demands that themselves cannot be further justified.

43. But this is a specious argument. Suppose that actions can be understood only by means of a socially given conceptual scheme – although exactly what this means itself needs explaining. Suppose also that moral ideas enter into this system. It does not follow that the corresponding moral demands must be acknowledged. Even if, in our society, the concept of justice, say, is indispensable for understanding actions, we need not therefore regard acting justly as something mandatory. In reply to the question 'Why should I act justly?', Norman claims to have shown the importance of the concept of justice for the system of moral concepts. But a person asking this question could not care less about the functional importance of the concept of justice. He needs to understand that justice, not 'justice,' is mandatory. Just as unconvincing are Norman's reasons for holding that it is impossible to prove this. In saying that the concept of justice plays this role in our conceptual system, one has already reached behind socially given norms in the way deemed impossible. If there is room for the knowledge of a system of moral concepts, and so, too, for the knowledge of the different systems which in different societies determine the fields of action in different ways, then there must also be room for comparison, critique, and justification of these concepts. At least there is no reason for this not to be so.[78]

44. Finally, Thomas Nagel's *The Possibility of Altruism* offers an argument for altruism being rationally mandatory. Altruism imposes the condition of objectivity on reasons for action. Formally, it says that reasons must not refer with a free variable to the agent in question. For example, someone's assertion that an action serves his own well-being is not an objective reason, for the full reason would be this: Everyone has reason to do whatever serves his well-being, 'his' referring as a free variable to the agent in question. In contrast, someone's claim that an action serves the well-being of at least one person does present an objective reason. The import of the objectivity condition is that the reasons for action must not be merely reasons for certain individuals but reasons for anyone to promote the events in question (X, 1).[79] The altruism requirement implies certain moral principles (I, 1; XIII, 1). The requirement itself cannot be further justified (I, 2; IV, 1), but it can be interpreted (IV, 1; XI, 1) as the practical expression of an idea that every rational agent has, namely, the idea of oneself as one person among others (IX, 4). What has to be shown, then, is that the unrelinquishable[80] idea of oneself as one person among others precludes the validity of merely subjective reasons for action (XI–XIII).[81] Thus, altruism, in requiring reasons to be objective, is a demand of rationality.

45. The idea of the argument is this: Whoever considers herself one person among others must be able to regard herself impersonally in all respects (XI, 3). So whatever she judges in employing token-reflexive expressions, in particular the expression 'I,' she must accept a judgment "to the same effect" about the situation but not containing any token-reflexives. In the case of a practical judgment, such as "I should get out of the building before the bomb explodes," this means two things. First, the person must acknowledge a universal practical judgment, one that holds in the same sense for everyone and from which, therefore, one can infer what someone in the described situation should do, without knowing one's own place in it. An example of such a universal judgment would be this: One should promptly leave a building threatening to explode (XI, 5).[82] Second, the person must consider the universal practical judgment a reason for acting, as good a reason as the personally formulated practical judgment (XI, 6–7). Whoever refuses to acknowledge a judgment fulfilling these two conditions thus rests content with subjective reasons for action and violates the requirement of altruism, abandoning the metaphysical idea of herself as one person among others.

46. It comes as a surprise that an insight that seems so trivial for our everyday understanding of the world, the insight that one is one person among others, should have such powerful implications. In fact, the argument rests on a confusion. Someone who considers herself a person among others may indeed have to regard all judgments she makes about herself as transferable, in the sense that everything she says of herself may also be meaningfully said of others. Whoever concludes "I should leave the building" would be untrue to the idea of herself as one person among others if she did not also grant as meaningful the judgment "Thomas Nagel should leave the building" or the judgment "Anyone should leave a building threatened by a bomb attack." But she need not herself acknowledge these judgments as valid; she must only grant that they are meaningful. She is not committed to accepting a universal practical judgment. The confusion may have been fostered by the ambiguity of 'apply' and 'applicable.' Judgments may indeed have to be "applicable in the same sense to oneself and to others" (XI, 5), if this means that a parallel judgment about others ought to be meaningful. But judgments need not "apply in the same sense to everyone" (XI, 5), that is, be true of everyone. Also ambiguous is the phrase "to apply it [a judgment] to oneself, conceived as merely one person among others" (XI, 5). This can simply mean 'apply it to oneself and further know that there are other persons besides oneself.' But it can also mean 'make the judgment about oneself on the grounds that it holds for all persons in the same situation.' The metaphysical idea requires judgments to be applicable to oneself as just one person among others in the sense of the first reading. It does not require judgments to be applicable to oneself as one person among others in the sense of the second reading, as Nagel claims. The choice between the two readings also decides whether Nagel is correct in holding that substantial moral demands follow from the principle of altruism. Certainly such demands do follow if altruism means acknowledging the universal practical judgment and regarding it as a reason for action. Then the subjective reasons, which each of us has on hand because they rest on natural desires and needs, will yield, in the manner sketched by Nagel (XIII, 1–2), generalizations that are reasons for actions aiming at the fulfillment of these needs for others as well as for ourselves.[83] But altruism in this sense does not follow from the idea of oneself as one person among others. The altruism that does follow, the idea that one's reasons for action can be stated in an impersonal way, remains formal. Whatever is set as a goal of action can in principle be regarded as a goal for everyone, and the reason for the action can be formulated as an objective reason.[84] Hence, there can be no question of substantial moral consequences.[85]

III. Contracts

47. The three theories to be discussed in this chapter pursue the same goal as did those theories covered in the preceding chapter. All aim at providing grounds for a positive answer to the question 'Should I be moral?' The theories discussed here are distinctive in seeking those grounds in the achievement of relations between individuals that can be described only by means of the concept of a contract. Contracts actually made by individuals offer one example of such relations. In addition, there are the cases of universal interest in a contract and of a contract into which all rational individuals will enter under certain ideal conditions, a fictitious contract. Ilting infers the validity of moral claims from actual contracts, Grice argues from a general interest in contracts, and Rawls argues from a fictitious contract. I shall consider these three approaches in reverse order.

48. One general remark at the outset: The attempt to reason from contractual relations between individuals to the validity of moral claims is something new. The classical tradition – Hobbes and Kant, for example – employed the notion of a contract in the context of law, not morality. The notion of a contract was to be of aid in answering the question of how the restriction of their freedom in a law-governed system of association could be justified to free individuals.[86] The justification was to be this: Given the choice, rational people will be prepared to limit the freedom of each person by means of a contract. This argument will have to be filled out by specifying the rational grounds for entering into a contract; whether or not the answer is satisfactory will depend on how these grounds are specified. The present context does not require such an evaluation, however. The two uses of contractual relations between individuals to demonstrate the validity of moral claims, on the one hand, and the legitimacy of legal systems, on the other, are two different things because legal systems differ from moral demands in ultimately threatening force in case of disobedience. Moreover, demonstrating the legitimacy of legal systems is not a stronger program whose completion would provide a demonstration of the validity of the corresponding moral claims as well. Contractual relations may well legitimize an order of association based on the means of force but not justify the corresponding moral claims (21). Hence, if the following shows that those arguments for the validity of moral demands that appeal to the contractual relations between individuals break down, this implies nothing about the prospects offered the philosophy of law by the notion of a contract.

49. The greater part of Rawls's considerations developed in *A Theory of Justice* may be passed over here, concerned as they are with the conditions for institutions holding justly. Our present concern is with moral demands in the narrower sense, the basis for our discussion thus far as well, such that a demand is moral only if directed at individuals and pertaining to their behavior. Rawls distinguishes two kinds of moral demands,[87] namely, to fulfill obligations and to fulfill natural duties. One enters obligations through voluntary action, and they exist based on institutions, such as an assumed office or a socially common practice, like promising. Duties do not exist based on institutions or practices, and they are not first assumed through voluntary action. All obligations fall under a principle, that of fairness. It states that one is obligated to do one's part as institutionally defined if one has

enjoyed the benefits of the arrangement in question and if
the latter is just. On the other hand, there are many principles of duty, corresponding to the various duties of aiding
the needy, avoiding unnecessary suffering, respecting others, and so forth. Rawls takes the most important of these
to be the duty of justice. It requires us to comply with just
institutions whose rules apply to us and, if these institutions do not yet exist, to help them come into being. For
both kinds of principles, fairness as well as the various
principles of duty, it must be shown that they would be
accepted by all members of a fictitious situation of original
choice under ideal conditions. The contractarian idea thus
enters at two points. Some moral demands grow out of
contracts, namely, some obligations, whereas others do
not, for example, all duties. But all moral principles, of
duty as well as of obligation, are to be justified based on
the fictitious agreement of all with all under ideal conditions. The fictitious character of the original agreement
allows this contract theory to assume duties holding unconditionally in the sense that their being in force does not
depend on the voluntary actions of individuals. The theory
claims that moral principles that would be chosen by all
participants in the ideal situation are valid principles.

50. It is difficult to see, however, how it could be
shown of a principle that it would be agreed to by rational
individuals under the ideal conditions of the original position. Even if the proof is weakened to showing that under
these conditions a given principle would be chosen from a
class of specified alternatives, instead of all possible alternatives,[88] the reservation remains; for how is one to know
how these rational individuals would choose? In the sense
defined by Rawls,[89] presumably none has ever been seen,
and in any case one has never been able to observe any in
the original position. The objection may seem unfair; for
according to Rawls, no empirical knowledge of human
beings, obviously lacking here, will decide which principles would be chosen in the original position, but only a
deduction from a description of the original position and
its rationally choosing individuals.[90] In fact, Rawls consid-

ers a strict deduction only an ideal, far outstripping the considerations he brings to bear.[91] What he does carry out in support of his claim that the stated moral principles would be chosen in the original position still seems especially inadequate.[92] Only the choice of the principle of justice gets justified, even if not independently, namely, in that it, unlike the choice of a utilitarian principle, preserves coherence with principles already chosen for institutions.[93] With the other principles of duty and the principle of fairness, Rawls is content to point out the utility of general compliance and the convenience of living in such a society; he does not consider principles that would prescribe that individuals behave differently.[94] Hence, there can be no question of his having proved that the moral principles would be chosen by all participants in the ideal situation.[95]

51. Yet assuming that this were proved, what remains above all unclear is the value of this claim. The fact that a principle would be selected by rational individuals in the original position does not entail its validity for us now. Fictitious individuals may choose what they will – what do we care? True, we ourselves would be these individuals if we stood in the idealized position of choosing, and we can consistently imagine being in this situation. But because we never actually find ourselves in this situation, the idea has no import for the question of the validity of moral demands.[96] Rawls takes up this natural objection only in a marginal way, so that we might suppose that his theory of justice simply does not aim at showing the validity of moral demands.[97] Thus, Höffe finds that Rawls has only reconstructed the moral point of view by means of game and decision theory.[98] If that is so, then the idea of the original position serves only to explicate moral demands, not to prove their validity, and reference to the uselessness of the idea for such a proof is beside Rawls's point. But if this is so, then Rawls's work generally is irrelevant to our question.

52. Yet it can be said against interpreting Rawls this way that he evidently does consider the objection relevant, even if he treats it only marginally. He writes:

It is natural to ask why, if this agreement is never actually entered into, we should take any interest in these principles, moral or otherwise. The answer is that the conditions embodied in the description of the original position are ones that we do in fact accept. Or if we do not, then perhaps we can be persuaded to do so by philosophical reflection. Each aspect of the contractual situation can be given supporting grounds. Thus what we shall do is to collect together into one conception a number of conditions on principles that we are ready upon due consideration to recognize as reasonable.[99]

What this passage means depends on what exactly these conditions are. On one reading, the conditions mentioned in the second sentence, those embodied in the description of the original position, would simply be the conditions of the original position, conditions that a state of affairs must satisfy so that it can qualify as an original position. But this reading is not compatible with the last sentence of the passage, which speaks of conditions not on situations but on principles. Moreover, on this reading, the second sentence does not give an answer to the question raised in the first sentence. That we accept the conditions of an original position, fulfilled by the original position described by Rawls, does not indicate any reason for the principles chosen there being valid or of concern to us in any other way. So the conditions must apply to principles, as the last sentence suggests, hence, in the present case, to moral principles. That the text immediately follows with "These constraints . . ." suggests interpreting these conditions as necessary. Then the answer given by the second sentence would run: "The original position embodies conditions the satisfaction of which we deem necessary for a principle chosen there to be morally valid." But on this reading, again the sentence does not really answer the question. Even if a moral principle, in order to be valid as such, would have to be chosen in the original position, this does not warrant conversely concluding that a principle that would be chosen is therefore morally valid. Hence, the conditions should be understood as sufficient. The second sentence then means: "The original position embodies conditions the satisfaction of which we deem sufficient for a moral principle chosen in it to be valid." But now the answer is tautological. We had asked why the choice of a principle in the original position entails its validity, and we are not helped by the answer that we do accept this inference. Some people do not accept it, and would have to be shown that accepting it is rational. The third sentence gives some prospect of such reasons being presented, and in the last paragraph of his book, Rawls says that the relevant "philosophical considerations" have been "occasionally introduced." But whichever passages he has in mind here, a cogent argument is not to be found among them.[100]

53. David A. J. Richards's theory of reasons for action[101] closely follows Rawls, at least so far as moral reasons are concerned, which alone concern us here. In Richards's account, too, something is a valid moral principle if under ideal conditions it would be agreed to by rational individuals as a rule for action.[102] On the basis of this criterion, he draws up a list of moral principles.[103] These are said to be valid to the extent that people have the concept of something like morality and have the requisite competence to act and to control their actions.[104] But it is still unclear why the choice of a principle in the original position confers validity on it.[105] Not even Rawls's "natural question" finds a place in Richards's account.[106]

54. Evidently, ideal contracts are too weak to prove the validity of moral demands. The contract theory developed by Geoffrey Russell Grice[107] returns from an ideal situation of rational individuals to our world[108] and bases the desired proof on a universally shared interest in contracts. The concept of 'interest' is ambiguous, however. Grice uses the word in the sense of what might be called 'objective interest.' If an action lies in someone's interest, then there are reasons for her doing it. She need not want to do it, nor even know the reasons for doing it.[109] Grice's thesis is this: If it lies in each person's interest to conclude a contract with everyone else to act a certain way, then acting this way is obligatory; that is to say, in the terms I have been using, the corresponding moral demand is valid. The argument is this: Assuming that it lies in the interest of each person to conclude a contract with everyone else to act a certain way, and assuming that acting this way is not obligatory, then *not* acting this way either is or is not obligatory. But it is impossible that not acting this way is obligatory; for by hypothesis, it lies in the interest of each to conclude a contract with everyone else to act this way, and hence it lies in the interest of each that acting this way is obligatory for all. If it were at the same time obligatory not to act this way, then this would be an obligation such that its existence would lie in no one's interest, and the existence of the opposite obligation would lie in every individual's interest; but there cannot be such an obligation. Hence, it is not obligatory not to act this way. There remains the possibility that neither acting this way nor not acting this way is obligatory; in other words, acting this way is morally neutral. A morally neutral way of acting is such that neither performing nor omitting the action harms others. But if neither performing nor omitting a kind of action harms others, it cannot lie in the interest of each person to bind all others by means of a contract to act this way – contrary to hypothesis. Hence, acting this way is not morally neutral. Hence, the assumption that acting this way is not obligatory is false. So it is obligatory. Any way of acting, then, such that it lies in everyone's interest to conclude a contract with everyone else to act this way, is therefore obligatory – which is what Grice had claimed.[110]

55. The argument uses two questionable premises. The first is that there can be no obligation such that the existence of its opposite would lie in everyone's interest. The premise rests on a previously stated general argument that if something is an obligation for everyone, then it must lie in everyone's interest. This argument proceeds by elimination. That something's being an obligation for everyone lies in no one's interest can be excluded from the outset, and that this lies in the interest of only some is also absurd because the principles of duty, by definition, cannot serve merely particular interests. Hence, it must lie in the interest of everyone.[111] But, first, it is unclear what 'interest' now means. What it means for an action to lie in some-one's interest has been explained (54). What it means to say that a state of affairs lies in someone's interest, such as the state of affairs of a certain way of acting's being obligatory for everyone, is not intelligible without further explana-tion. Let us be content, however, with vaguely under-standing talk of a state of affairs lying in someone's interest to mean that the person will benefit if that state obtains. Still, it is not convincing to say that the existence of a universal obligation must lie in everyone's interest. We cannot exclude the possibility that no one has an interest in it, that is to say, that no one benefits from the existence of the obligation. And even if there is an interest in a certain universal obligation, that interest need not be universally shared. Suppose that there is a moral obligation to non-violence: Although the existence of this obligation in the case of an oppressive state serves the interests of its rulers, this fact does not affect the claim of the command.[112] Du-ties can be altogether indifferent to the interests of the individuals they address; the existence of an obligation may happen to meet or run counter to the interests of either some or all of those concerned. For all his criticism of utilitarianism,[113] Grice here succumbs to utilitarian prejudices in not considering this possibility.[114]

56. Also problematic is the premise Grice uses to ex-clude the possibility that the given way of acting is morally neutral. This is the premise that a type of action is morally neutral only if neither acting this way nor not acting this way harms others by virtue of being an action of this type. In brief: If a certain way of acting is morally neutral, then other people are harmed neither by performance nor by omission of the corresponding actions. It is also assumed, therefore, that if others are harmed by the performance of an action, then that type of action is not morally neutral. In this case, it is also surely not a duty. Hence, it is morally forbidden. Similarly for the opposite case: If others are harmed by omission of an action, then that type of action is not morally neutral. But surely it is not forbidden. So it is morally obligatory. Thus, the premise of the argument, supplemented only by an unproblematic clause, already implies that what harms others is morally forbidden, and that omission of what harms others is morally required. But these themselves are moral principles, and indeed utilitarian ones again, whose validity we had to demonstrate.

57. Karl-Heinz Ilting bases his attempt "towards a justification of practical statements" – the subtitle of his article "Acknowledgment" – on the strongest of contractarian foundations, namely, contracts actually concluded between individuals. He concedes that only a narrow spectrum of practical statements can be justified this way. Many statements for which we may desire justification definitely cannot be justified on the basis of actual contracts between individuals. This will especially be the case for many moral demands. In any event, we need concern ourselves not with the scope but with the structure and soundness of Ilting's argument for the validity of at least some moral demands.

58. The argument rests on an analysis of the concept of a contract. The analysis uses, besides the ordinary logical vocabulary, the primitive notion of a volition. A statement expresses a volition if it presents a state of affairs as one "of which the speaker desires that it be realized."[115] The word 'ought' serves to indicate the volitional sense. Predication, on the other hand, presents a state of affairs as one that is realized.[116] If the state of affairs that is the object of a volition consists in the person addressed bringing about a certain condition, then the ought-statement is called an imposition. To accept an imposition is "to adopt the thought contained in it and to act accordingly."[117] The acceptance of an imposition is logically and causally independent of the imposition itself and is up to the person at whom the imposition is directed. For a contract, "there must be a mutual imposition and a mutual acceptance of the imposition, with each reciprocally conditioning the other. The participants must agree that this condition is to regulate their actions."[118] A contract is to be understood as an ought-statement (i.e., as the expression of the volition of a state of affairs). Its form is this: If the person addressed imposes on the speaker that he bring about a certain condition, then the speaker accepts this imposition. The acceptance of an ought-statement that is a contract is called an 'acknowledgment.' If and only if the person addressed and the person speaking have acknowledged an ought-statement does it become a norm for their actions. Should either person furnish under these conditions the contractually stipulated performance, then the demand on the other to do his part is no mere imposition that he "may accept or reject as he pleases. It becomes a claim which he has already acknowledged as a condition on his actions. He has, in other words, obligated himself to fulfilling this claim."[119] Whether or not all obligations are of this type, as Ilting suggests, we need not decide. At least demands that can be based this way on contracts are supposed to be proved valid for this reason.

59. The grounds of this proof are unclear, however. The idea evidently is that the person on whom the demand is made can no longer reject the imposition, because he has already accepted it in concluding the contract. He has implicitly accepted it in concluding the contract, just as a person who grants one claim implicitly grants another logically contained in the first. This reading is supported by the volition of the contract being a volition of a conditional relationship. We have, that is, an argument by modus ponens. In concluding the contract, one accepts the volition of 'If A, then B.' But now A. So one has also accepted the volition of B.

60. But, in reality, these considerations do not apply to contracts. Contracts do not obtain between two persons once each bindingly declares his willingness to accept a certain imposition from the other. Such declarations may be necessary for concluding contracts, but they do not suffice. Suppose I see someone I know approaching. Expecting that he will make a certain request, I say to my fellow traveler that I will fulfill the request. My approaching acquaintance does the same on his part. But one would not then say that he and I have concluded a contract with each other. Missing is not only the one party's binding declaration of will to the other, rather than simply to a third party; also missing is a reference in the one declaration of will to the content of the other: what Ilting calls the 'reciprocal conditioning' of impositions and acceptance. But Ilting's argument does not turn on this 'reciprocal conditioning,' whatever its precise analysis may be. The argument concerns only one party's binding declaration of will to fulfill a certain demand made by the other. The possibly one-sided declaration of will to this effect would alone allow one to infer a currently valid obligation by modus ponens. So what Ilting presents is not really an analysis of what it is to acknowledge shared norms. It is not a shared norm that my acquaintance and I are following when each of us lives up to his own declaration of will. We are doing different things. We have not agreed to any shared rule prescribing the fulfillment of both our requests. Ilting's analysis would have to cover the 'reciprocal conditioning' before he could speak of a shared norm of our actions.

61. One's binding declaration of will to fulfill another's demand is not tantamount to entry into a contract. It is the promise of something. Promises, not contracts, are what Ilting is discussing. His argument is this: A certain performance is promised for a certain case. The case is that of the other person making a certain demand. The performance consists in fulfilling this demand. In promising, one accepts a volition of the form 'If A, then B.' Now A; that is, the other person makes the demand in question. So one has implicitly already accepted the volition of B, that is, fulfillment of the demand, and cannot deny an obligation to this effect.

62. In relating the argument to promises, one may also extend its scope. More moral demands may be justifiable this way than through contracts (57). On the other hand, the argument runs into a number of difficulties. In the first place, someone might dispute the validity of inferring by modus ponens in this context and insist that she had merely acknowledged the volition: 'If A, then B.' She may concede that the volition is fulfilled just in case 'If A, then B,' is true, as Ilting states.[120] She may also grant that A, that only the truth of B is missing for the truth of 'If A, then B,' and that realizing B rests in her hands. Nevertheless, she claims that she can rightly reject the imposition of doing B because she never agreed to acknowledge the volition of B itself. She behaves as obstinately as the tortoise in its dispute with Achilles.[121] To the tortoise, however, we can reply as follows: If you mean by 'if' what we all mean, you have to accept modus ponens, for that is the rule whereby 'if' obtains its meaning.[122] Our friend is not caught by this answer, because ordinary usage does not as clearly fix the meaning of 'if' for volitions as it does for predications. Prichard considered this so great a difficulty that he even refused to admit volitions involving conditional states of affairs.[123] But the matter requires more extended semantic considerations than can be pursued here. So I shall leave open whether or not the objection can be met satisfactorily.

63. Second, someone could claim that in promising she had indeed acknowledged her volition to perform the action, but that in the meantime she has retracted this acknowledgment. She thus considers the formerly existing obligation canceled and herself free again to do as she pleases with the imposition. Ilting counters with the distinction "between acknowledgment of norms and other, non-binding declarations of will: the acknowledgment of any norm already presupposes a previous acknowledgment of a 'basic norm' to the effect that acknowledgment of a norm is to be regarded as an act of will which henceforward may be validly held against this will itself."[124] Habermas finds such a basic norm absurd because "the validity of norms cannot be grounded on an obligation to oneself not to change them."[125] Still, it does not seem hopeless to modify the basic norm so as to allow sensible changes in already concluded contracts without thereby robbing them of binding force. More serious is the circularity of the construction. Someone who in acknowledging the basic norm declares his promise forever valid can nevertheless in any given situation recall his acknowledgment of the basic norm, so that he can also retract his promise at any given time. To assure us of his lasting acknowledgment of the basic norm, he would have to acknowledge a basic basic norm, and so on. In fact, none of the norms can be made permanently binding in this way. Ilting does give reasons, Hobbesian ones, supposedly making acknowledgment of the basic norm advisable.[126] These may even be good reasons, but that is beside the point. The issue is not whether it is advisable to leave a condition in which there are no agreements, but how we are able to leave it. We do not see how, so long as the demands arising from promises have not been ensured lasting validity.

64. Finally, the most serious objection. Ilting tried to demonstrate the validity of moral demands. True, certain restrictions had to be imposed: Ilting's contract theory is concerned not with contracts but with promising (61), and the demonstration may not cover many moral demands (57). Still, a demonstration was supposed to be given: Some moral demands are valid because, in promising, the person they address has made them valid. So the demand is now valid because it has been valid all along, and it became valid because the person in question made it valid in promising. But anyone seeking a demonstration of the validity of moral demands will find quite strong the premise that in promising, one makes a demand valid. He would like to know how this comes about. First a demand was not valid, and now it is, and the person it addresses has brought this about through certain actions. The question is how he did this. We would like to watch his hands in the act, as it were, so that we may understand how this result comes to pass. It is only when we can explain how certain actions succeed in making a demand valid that reference to these actions will be able to support an argument designed to demonstrate the validity of the demand.

IV. Promising

65. We next consider the attempt to demonstrate the validity of some moral demands on the grounds that the person they address has made a promise corresponding to the demand. Now, it may be questioned whether matters do stand as just described, that is, whether in promising one already makes valid a moral demand for the corresponding action. Or, because in the following I shall say that an obligation is incumbent on a person if that person falls under a valid moral demand, it may be questioned whether in promising one already posits an obligation. Many authors alternatively justify the obligations arising from promising by using a moral principle that is valid independently of the act of promising. This may simply be the moral principle of keeping a promise, as with Hare,[127] or a moral principle applicable to a wider range of actions, such as avoiding the harm to others that would arise from disappointing their reasonable expectations, as with Ardal.[128] Promising something, then, means not so much obligating oneself to do something as just voluntarily placing oneself in a situation in which one stands under certain obligations. The two are not the same. For example, a driver starting his car does not thereby obligate himself to obey the traffic regulations, but he does fall under this obligation. But this recourse to an independent moral principle ruins the prospects for demonstrating the validity of moral demands in a nontrivial way based on promises, for the validity of this moral principle is equally at issue. So promising helps us in our quest for a proof of validity only if under certain conditions we do activate moral demands on action in promising, without further having to appeal to some independent moral principle. In more familiar terms: Promising helps us prove the validity of moral demands only if it is a tautology that one is under an obligation to keep one's promise.[129]

66. The claim that 'promises ought to be kept' is a tautology has been most staunchly defended by John Searle.[130] Critics of his work have rejected his arguments on a number of grounds. Their criticisms suggest the following objection to the foregoing argument: It may indeed be the case that a deduction of the validity of moral demands has some chance of succeeding only if 'promises ought to be kept' is a tautology; then so much the worse for this deduction, for the dispute with Searle shows this claim to be false. But actually the dispute shows nothing of the kind. To justify this verdict, I investigate some important contributions to this discussion (67–72). I hope to show that although Searle's argumentation is brought down by one of the objections raised, we may still regard 'promises ought to be kept' as a tautology.

67. In his work, Searle sets out to refute Hume's law, as it is called:[131] No ought-statement can be derived from is-statements alone. Searle's counterexample consists in the following five statements:

(1) Jones uttered the words "I hereby promise to pay you, Smith, five dollars."
(2) Jones promised to pay Smith five dollars.
(3) Jones placed himself under (undertook) an obligation to pay Smith five dollars.
(4) Jones is under an obligation to pay Smith five dollars.
(5) Jones ought to pay Smith five dollars.

Searle claims that each statement in the sequence logically follows from its predecessor if further premises are granted that are no more ought-statements than is statement 1:

(1a)   Under certain conditions C, anyone who utters the words (sentence) "I hereby promise to pay you, Smith, five dollars" promises to pay Smith five dollars.

(1b)   Conditions C obtain.

(2a)   All promises are acts of placing oneself under (undertaking) an obligation to do the thing promised.

(4a)   Other things are equal.

Basically, two objections have been raised against Searle's claim. The first notes that the statement '1a and 2a' is a synthetic moral principle, and the second finds an ought-statement in the ceteris paribus clause 4a. I shall consider Hare's version of the first objection[132] and James and Judith Thomson's statement of the second.[133]

68. To simplify the argument, Hare conjoins premises 1a and 2a:

(1a*)   Under certain conditions C, anyone who utters the words (sentence) "I hereby promise to pay you, Smith, five dollars" places himself under (undertakes) an obligation to pay Smith five dollars.

Searle considers 2a a tautology and 1a an empirical statement about English usage. So he would also regard 1a* as an empirical statement about English. Hare's argument is supposed to show that 1a* is neither an empirical statement about English nor a tautology. He makes use of an analogy already introduced by Searle, that of 1a* to a rule in a game. Just as

(1a′*)   Whenever a player satisfies conditions E, he is obliged to leave the field

could be laid down as a rule for baseball, so 1a* is a rule for the game called 'promising.' The rules of baseball cannot be all tautological, for otherwise they would be rules not for playing but for speaking about the game. For the same reason, these rules cannot be statements about linguistic usage or prescriptions for it: "They are about how a game is, or is to be, played."[134] The same applies to promising. Statement 1a* cannot be a tautology, for being a rule in the game, it concerns actions. For the same reason, 1a* can be neither an empirical claim about nor a prescription for linguistic usage. The argument goes awry, however, in forgetting the analogy between baseball and promising that it had just invoked; for as Hare says, one move in the promising game is to say, 'I promise, etc.'[135] Just because the rules of a game concern how something is or should be played, the rules of the game 'promising' concern how certain expressions, in particular the sentence 'I promise,' are or should be used. The fact that rules concern how a game is or should be played may indeed, in the case of baseball, be a good reason for saying that they do not concern linguistic usage, but not so in the case of promising. Promising, unlike baseball, is a language game.

69. But Hare still has two other arguments against assuming that 1a* is an empirical statement about English; alternatively, they may be considered two versions of the same argument. The first:

> Nor are either of these merely remarks about word usage. For it is a necessary condition for the adoption of these performative expressions that certain synthetic constitutive (and not merely linguistic) rules be also adopted, thus creating the institution within which the expressions have meaning.[136]

What this is supposed to mean is not clear. It could be read as follows: Whoever uses, say, the expression 'I promise' regards rule 1a* as valid. It is a synthetic and constitutive rule, not just a linguistic rule. In regarding it as valid, one creates the institution under which the expression 'I promise' has meaning. But the first of these statements is false – after all, a person may use the expression mistakenly. The second statement commits a petitio principii – that 1a* is not a linguistic rule was to be shown. We still do not understand the third statement; what it means to say that an institution is created by the acknowledgment of a rule is quite unclear.

70. The second additional argument runs as follows: Perhaps we can understand 1a* as a statement about English usage. But then it is an anthropological statement. It informs us that English speakers have the expression 'I promise' in their language, that they use it to make promises, and that sufficiently many of them acknowledge the rules of the institution of promising. So understood, however, 1a* does not allow a derivation of Searle's statements 3–5, but only statements such as 'English speakers believe that 3 is true'. The desired moral consequences can be drawn only if 1a, interpreted in light of 2a, is understood as expressing the speaker's own acknowledgment of the rules of the institution of promising, which are moral rules.[137] But in fact there is no reason to think that 1a*, taken as a statement about usage, would be an anthropological statement, one about the curious practices and moral opinions of English speakers. The statement does not say that they believe, or act under the belief, that in using a certain expression one assumes what they call an obligation. It says that in using this expression, one does assume an obligation. The statement is a piece of linguistic theory, but not of anthropology. English speakers may in fact promise only deceitfully or not at all; the fact remains that by using 'I promise' in English, one promises, under certain conditions. Consider a parallel case, that of declarations of war. Nowadays the custom is falling into desuetude – wars are waged undeclared. Even so, it remains true that in saying, for example, 'We declare war, etc.' one does declare war. Accordingly, 1a* does not enable us to derive any statement about how English speakers regard Searle's statements 3–5. On the other hand, there is no reason to take 1a* as expressing the speaker's acknowledgment of the rules of promising. The speaker and her beliefs are no more the subject matter of the statement than are English speakers in general. If it is maintained against this that the speaker's acknowledgment of the rules can be seen from her having made this statement, then it is difficult to see how this fact, if it is one, can justify drawing moral consequences from the statement that otherwise could not be drawn. After all, what follows from a statement depends on what it says, not on the attitude of the speaker it reveals.

71. The discussion starting from Searle's work has also been confused because Searle mistakes the import of the objections made. He takes Hare's objection seriously and tries, though without success, to meet it.[138] On the other hand, he declares irrelevant James and Judith Thomson's critique of the ceteris paribus clause, although that critique wrecks his program.[139] To establish the inference from 4 to 5, the clause must say this: In the given case, there are no compelling reasons for that particular obligation not to hold. But this is itself a premise having moral content. Searle tries to escape the objection by explicating 5 as follows:

(5′)   As regards his obligation to pay Smith five dollars, Jones ought to pay Smith five dollars.[140]

But 5′ says the same as

(5*)   Other things being equal, Jones ought to pay Smith five dollars

which Searle has already employed in his original version of the argument.[141] James and Judith Thomson have already countered this strategy: 5* is analytic, at least if the law of excluded middle is.[142] That analytic ought-statements follow from is-statements is of no interest, however.[143]

72. James and Judith Thomson test just the inference from 4 to 5.[144] Yet it is questionable whether the ceteris paribus clause properly belongs at this point in Searle's argument. No doubt the clause must somewhere be introduced into the argument in order to preserve its validity; for sometimes we do express ourselves in the way that is usual for promising, and the normal boundary conditions also obtain. That is, statements like 1 and 1b in Searle's argument are true, and yet we ought not to do the particular action; that is, a statement like 5 in Searle's argument is not true. This always happens, for example, when the action supposedly promised is itself morally objectionable. In such cases, the ceteris paribus clause functions to block the inference to a statement like 5. But the inference can be

blocked at an earlier or later point. If we place the clause
where Searle directs us to, between 4 and 5, then we must
describe as follows the case in which a morally objectionable action appears to be promised: A person not only has
expressed herself in the way that is usual in promising but
also has actually made a promise; she has assumed an obligation and is now obligated to do the action in question,
only she ought not to do it. But an assertion that a person
is obligated to do something and yet ought not to do it is
difficult to tolerate in ordinary language. In support of his
construction, Searle notes that an obligation has to exist in
the first place if it is to be overridden.[145] But this is to take
'overriding' too literally. An obligation that is overridden
is really an obligation that does not exist, and the realization that one obligation is overridden by another is the
realization that it is erroneous to assume, on the basis of
certain features of the situation, that there is such a thing as
the first obligation. Now, we can easily avoid this jarring
talk by pushing the ceteris paribus clause farther back. But
we do best to place it right up front, between 1 and 2, and
not regard the alleged promise to do something morally
objectionable as really being a promise. This is best, because we then avoid the new burden of having to say of
someone that she has assumed an obligation, but is not
obligated, or of having to say that she has made a promise,
and yet has not assumed any obligation. In comparison,
saying that someone has uttered 'I promise, etc.' and yet
has not made a promise is much less odd. Moreover, talking this way is unavoidable in some cases anyway; for if
the conditions C to which Searle refers in 1a and 1b are not
fulfilled, we must similarly say that a person who utters 'I
promise, etc.' has not made a promise. No one has as yet
exhaustively spelled out conditions C. Hence, we do best
to adjoin to conditions C the condition imposed by the
ceteris paribus clause.[146] Clearly, 1b will then no longer be
decidable by empirical means only, but will require a moral evaluation as well. But this does no harm, because
Searle's derivation of an ought statement from mere is-
statements, for the sake of which derivation he wanted to
preserve the empirical character of 1b, is untenable. To be

sure, none of this proves that 'promises ought to be kept' *is* a tautology. It only shows that 'promises ought to be kept' can be regarded as a tautology and that we stay closest to linguistic usage in so regarding it.

73. But to regard as a tautology the statement that in promising, one assumes an obligation to carry out what is promised is not yet to understand what the statement says. It may be true that we ordinarily use the concept of promising in such a way that whoever promises freely activates a moral demand on herself; and using the concept of promising this way, we may ordinarily not run into any difficulties. Nevertheless, we do not understand how a person is supposed to activate a moral demand on herself by means of a voluntary action. That was the problem raised earlier (64). It is not the problem of what sort of actions these are and what conditions they require for success. This problem Searle has satisfactorily resolved: An example of such an action is the utterance of 'I promise,' and the conditions for success are the normal conditions for communication, among others. The problem is, rather, how to explain that such actions under such conditions do succeed in establishing an obligation. Prichard has noted the paradox of this idea:

> In promising, agreeing, or undertaking to do some action we seem to be creating or bringing into existence the obligation to do it, so much so that promising seems just to *be* binding ourselves, i.e. making ourselves bound, to do it, and the statement 'I ought to keep a promise,' like 'I ought not to steal,' seems a mere pleonasm. . . . Yet an obligation seems a fact of a kind which it is impossible to create or bring into existence.[147]

If it is maintained, against the first part of the dilemma, that 'promises ought to be kept' is not analytic, then promising involves not creating but assuming an obligation that addresses all persons meeting a certain condition. In this case, in promising, we enter the domain of application of a certain obligation – an obligation, however, existing independently of the act of promising (65). Prichard

himself finally opts for a solution of this sort, even if with
great misgivings. He supposes that there is a prior agreement to the effect that uttering 'I promise' or the like
involves assuming an obligation to do the particular action.[148] Rawls and Richards follow suit, except that in
place of a prior agreement they introduce the moral fairness principle, agreed to by rational individuals in a fictitious convocation.[149] But these proposals run into the difficulty mentioned earlier. Whether moral demands,
including the demand to do what has been promised, are
valid and whether an obligation does arise from Prichard's
prior agreement or from Rawls's and Richards's fictitious
one (51) are precisely the questions here (65). An intelligible notion of promising, not weighted down by strong
moral presuppositions, can be upheld only if the other half
of the dilemma is erroneous.

74. We are led to ask, then, why an obligation should
be something of which it does not make sense to say that it
is brought into existence. Prichard only hints at an answer.
The passage I quoted earlier continues:

> There are, no doubt, certain facts which we do seem
> able to create. If, e.g., I make someone angry, I ap-
> pear to bring into existence the fact that he is angry.
> But the fact that I am bound to do some action seems
> no more one of these than does the fact that the
> square of three is odd.

Granting that it is meaningless or at least 'very' false to say
of someone that he has brought it about that the square of
three is an odd number, we still face this question: By
virtue of what property does a moral fact (i.e., the fact that
a certain moral demand on someone is valid) resemble a
mathematical fact in that we cannot speak of bringing it
about? It may be replied that a moral fact, like a mathematical fact, is an ideal fact, and so cannot be brought
about through action. Yet, in a sense, all facts are ideal;
they cannot be seen. In another sense, however, such that
facts are ideal if their existence is determinable by nonem-
pirical means, applying the predicate causes so much difficulty that we gain nothing by it. It is not clear in just what

sense mathematical truths are inaccessible to empirical verification; after all, we can use matchsticks in learning how to calculate. On the other hand, even if empirical means do not suffice to determine the existence of an obligation, they are still relevant in the matter. For example, whether or not the sounds 'I promise' have been made does make a difference. If, finally, one calls ideal those facts that exist independently of time, then a moral fact is not ideal. A person can begin and cease to be obligated; so why should he not bring it about himself? Prichard fails to explain, then, why an obligation is a fact that cannot sensibly be said to be brought about.

75. Here is a different explanation of this way of talking being indeed meaningless, and Prichard's paradox holding. A person falls under an obligation, by my definition (65), if some moral demand on her is valid. Sometimes she will not want to fulfill the demand. Whether in the end she actually fulfills it or not, in such a case the moral demand is opposed to what she herself wants. This is, if not the normal case for moral demands, still the case in which they acquire their characteristic weight, and hence it decides their import. In the case of promising, a moral demand is valid only by virtue of the person who promises making it valid through her own free action. But I do not see how what exists only because of her will can now acquire an independent standing and turn against her will. Sometimes one does regret one's actions, so that, it could be said, one's present will turns against one's former will. But this way of talking is imprecise; in such cases, I am confronted with particular states of the world that I have brought about myself and could have prevented. But the promise did not change the world, apart from the negligible effects of sounds or marks. Through promising, nothing happens that makes difficult or impossible an action I would otherwise prefer to perform. Promising only establishes the demand to omit the action. But since the demand is in force only because I have placed it in force, and since, on the other hand, it is only a demand, not an actual state of the world, that can at most be changed but not recalled, I do not see how the demand can continue as a claim against a

will that has changed, rather than simply lose its force and
dissolve before the new will. I do not see how the prior
resolution can fix an obligation that exists and endures like
a thing, at last opposing itself to my will.[150] The demand
to do what is promised stands opposed to my will in the
name of my will. But one would think that against my
present will, my prior will has no force, and that a mere
change of will cancels the old demand.[151] The concession
of its continued validity is an unintelligible regression to
self-imposed minority.

76. The point can be made clearer by considering some
English expressions used in speaking of obligations. One
group of expressions are based on the idea of obligation as
a burden. In promising, it is said, we 'undertake' to do
something, and the obligation is then 'incumbent' upon
the person who has 'placed himself under it.' It can therefore 'weigh' upon him; it can be 'heavy' or 'pressing.'
Carrying such a burden, we cannot do certain things we
otherwise could. Obligated to do something, one ought
not to do something (namely, omit the action in question),
even if nothing else speaks against doing it. But in the case
of promising, the metaphor proves misplaced, and this
shows that in promising, what the metaphor stands for –
obligation – is as unintelligible as the metaphor. The metaphor is misplaced because the alleged burden can neither
stand ready prior to promising nor come into existence
through the act of promising. It does not stand ready, in
the way that other burdens stand ready to be taken up,
because there is no obligation prior to the act of promising. One cannot 'take on' an obligation through promising, because there is nothing here that can be 'taken on.'
Nor does the obligation come into existence through the
act of promising, for it cannot be produced; an obligation
is not something that can be made from other things by
promising. The promise, then, would have to create the
obligation from nothing. But such talk of creation is unintelligible. We understand what it means to make something out of something. We do not understand what it
means to 'call something into existence.' In just the same
way, we do not understand what it means to 'call an obli-

gation into existence.' Thus, the idea of obligation as a burden can in no way be intelligibly applied to promising, and whoever groans under such a burden should not be told that he has placed it upon himself, but rather that his shoulders are in fact free.

77. Another group of expressions present the person under obligation as bound. In promising, it is said, we 'bind' ourselves, so that we are 'bound' to do a certain thing, or, as Kleist's Prince Friedrich von Homburg was told when set free on parole, "Your word is a fetter, too."[152] In fact, the very word 'obligation' originally expressed this idea of being tied to something.[153] This metaphor is an old and customary one in several languages, for English so much so that its metaphorical character is hardly noticeable any longer.[154] It fits obligations for the same reason the preceding metaphor did: Whoever is bound can no longer do certain things. Like 'burden' earlier, the 'bind' in promising turns out to be a misplaced metaphor, for here the bind is supposed to be the work of the one who becomes bound, the idea being that he binds himself. But whoever binds himself can release himself, and so is not really bound. Of course, a person can lock himself up and throw away the key, but that amounts to changing the world so that he can no longer do certain things. Such is not the case in promising, however; promises do not hinder actions (75). In promising, we are supposed to bind ourselves without the external fetter of an altered state of the world. But this is unintelligible. The point is not that it would be unwise to proceed this way; we simply do not understand how someone could possibly become bound solely by himself. Whatever is being withheld from the person bound can at any time be obtained by that very same person, he being the one who does the binding. We cannot take freedom away from ourselves; it can only be taken from us. The obligation arising from promising is indeed intelligible if there is some higher authority conferring validity on the demand for the action in question, for example, if a god, or that mortal god Leviathan,[155] watches over the sanctity of contracts and promises, or if valid moral principles lend obligatory force to the given word.

But that does not help us understand how an obligation can arise from the act of promising alone, and that was our question (65). After all, some higher authority's claim to obedience is no less questionable than the claim of the particular promise that it is supposed to support.

78. So the result is this: That promises give rise to obligations is part of the idea of promising. Nevertheless, this way of talking remains unintelligible. Our current concept of promising remains unintelligible. But saying this provokes the question of how, then, we should understand what we call 'promising.' After all, it will be said, there is such a thing as one person promising something to another. And it is good that there is such a thing. We are helped in living and working together by the fact that in promising, we make ourselves dependable for one another. But to answer this point, we should first remember that in fact we rather seldom formally promise something to another person (i.e., with utterances like 'promise,' 'I give my word,' or 'I obligate myself'). In supplying reliable knowledge about our future actions, we can dispense with promising, because we often achieve that goal in other ways. Most of the time we simply say what we intend to do, and usually this is reliable enough. True, it is difficult to demarcate which of our utterances already count as promises and which do not; for sometimes we employ expressions in promising that as a rule do not indicate an undertaking but normally serve to communicate an intention.[156] For example, if you tell your friend, "I'm going to Italy, and I'll bring back a bottle of Orvieto for you," your friend may reply, "Do you promise?" – having presumed that the statement was not yet a promise.[157] But he may also ask you on your return for the promised wine, having presumed that a promise had already been made.[158] So the line between promising and communicating intentions is not sharp.[159] Now, such difficulties of demarcation crop up for many concepts. That they crop up here is not a sufficient reason for obliterating the conceptual distinction altogether. But the absence of a sharp demarcation will suggest this way out to someone led by the preceding considerations to question the intelligibility of the very concept of promising. So the answer to the question raised at the beginning of this section is this: In a strict sense, there is no such thing as one person promising something to another, given, that is, that to promise is to posit an obligation. We do something else when we do what is ordinarily called 'promising.' We communicate to somebody that we intend to do a certain thing. Or, one might say, we announce to somebody that we are going to do it.[160] That words are fetters is superstition.

79. It may seem absurd on the one hand to claim that assuming an obligation belongs to the concept of promising and on the other to declare this concept unintelligible. After all, it must be intelligible to the extent that the first claim can be made. But intelligibility to this extent is not intelligibility enough, for what is said to belong to the very concept of something may itself fail to make sense, and that is the case here. In fact, it is not rare that we want to say two such apparently contradictory things, namely, whenever we reject a network of concepts as a whole while knowing well enough how to move within it. Thus, someone could state what God is – say the creator of the world – and then add that the idea of a creation is unintelligible, and hence the idea of God as well. It would not be absurd to talk this way. True, even people convinced by the argument against obligations as arising from promises may still have difficulty in concluding the nonexistence of promises. Rather, they may plead for describing the matter as follows: So-called promises really are promises, but it is not part of the concept of a promise that it give rise to obligations. But misunderstanding and specious reasoning will be less encouraged if we abide by the description first offered: Promising is assuming an obligation, but there is no such thing as promising. Strictly, then, we should speak only of alleged or so-called promises when referring to what is ordinarily called a promise. In the following, I shall avoid this awkward usage and simply call 'promising' what is ordinarily so called, because the explanation given here should prevent any misunderstanding.

80. It will be asked, then, Why do people relatively often keep their promises, if in promising they did not assume any obligations? In many cases, the reasons for making a promise also speak in favor of keeping it. Someone wishing to please a spouse by promising to do the cooking one evening usually does well to carry out this promise.[161] True, things do not always turn out that way. Sometimes, promising by itself has the desired effect, and performance can be left out. Having solicited customers by promising prompt service, often you may save yourself the trouble of actually providing that service, because most of your customers will retain you anyway. So, it will be further asked, why do people fairly often keep their promises even in such cases (i.e., against their interests) if, in promising, they have only told someone what they intend to do? Precisely because, in promising, they told someone what they intended to do. Keeping this in mind, we see that in many cases, performance really lies in the interest of the one who promises. We often find it advisable to carry out a previously declared intention, even if with regret. We may wish to avoid problems with those who would be harmed by our failure to perform; we may be too lazy or cowardly to go through a scene with them. Or we may wish to spare them harm and do what we said for their own sake. Or we may value being considered in the future as reliable. Reasons of this sort often recommend doing what was promised. Now, it may be asked why people still bother to communicate their intentions and aims to others if, because of this communication, they may later be required to perform actions that normally would not be in their interest. But the answer to this is simple: People only run the risk of later finding themselves in such a predicament if it is currently important to them to communicate their intentions or aims to others, and often it is important to them.

81. What I have been saying about promising differs, despite some similarities, from what utilitarian theories tell us.[162] The latter deny any difference between promising and declaring one's intentions. On the other hand, they acknowledge a moral demand to keep one's promises, as part of the general moral demand not to harm others by disappointing their justified expectations. But concerning the first point, the conceptual difference is obvious. Promising something means setting an obligation for oneself; declaring an intention does not mean this. In declaring an intention, one at most enters the domain in which some general moral demand applies (65), for example, the obligation to avoid disappointing others whenever possible. The utilitarian attempt to explain the obligation arising from promises runs aground on our ordinary idea of promising. The objection often raised against that account remains convincing, namely, that promising places specific moral demands in force that are not reducible to considerations of utility.[163] Better we grant, as I propose, that this is indeed our concept of promising, but then dismiss it as unintelligible. Concerning the second point: Reference to a higher moral demand does not bring us any further in the present context, for the validity of such demands is itself at issue.

82. What I have said about promising is also supported by the fact, noted by Narveson, that in ordinary usage we do not treat promises as inviolable:

> In fact, people break promises without qualms when they are of very minor importance and when there is reasonable certainty that the other party won't mind or 'will understand.'[164]

Narveson himself sees here an effective argument for the utilitarian theory of promising. In any case, this is not so. For example, Melden's theory of promising, which proceeds from the idea of a moral community formed by two parties, also does justice to this fact.[165] The best explanation assumes that no moral demand to keep promises is valid, but that whenever keeping the promise is required, it is required for just that sort of reason that in cases other than promising leads us to think that a certain action is required. Thus, in Warnock's example,[166] if I have promised to bring somebody a certain book, but in the meantime he has already received a copy from someone else, then we are inclined to say that my obligation ceases because my friend could hardly complain over an undelivered book if he already has a copy in hand.[167] True, some people still would complain; but in promising, we would feel more strongly obligated to such people. Similarly, an obligation may continue to exist, even though the matter has already taken care of itself, if our relation to the person promised is especially formal. Such particulars do not conform to the utilitarian picture, because in these cases the person suffers no harm from omission. They do conform to my picture. Promises contribute to the understanding we reach with one another, and we find it necessary to carry out our promises just as we regard it as necessary to do things we do not enjoy doing in order to preserve this understanding – in short, to have our peace.[168] So it is no wonder that the extent to which we regard ourselves as bound to a promise depends on the understanding partly formed by that promise.

83. My proposal also does justice to the case that creates difficulty for both Narveson's utilitarian theory and Melden's 'moral community,' namely, the deathbed promise.[169] Now, the deathbed itself, that is, the circumstance that a promise was made to a dying person, is of no interest. A promise is always made to someone whose situation is among the considerations leading to the promise being made. But that situation has different imports in different cases, and deathbed promises and promises made under the threat of death may define the extremes. What is of interest is that at some point soon afterward, the person is dead to whom the promise was made. A moral demand to fulfill the promise based, as in Narveson, on the utility of the person promised or, as in Melden, on his status as a moral agent would become moot on the death of that person, which does not tally with the fact that sometimes we do not find ourselves relieved of our promises by the death of the person promised. Warnock, on the other hand, in explaining the duty to keep a promise as the duty to be truthful (i.e., the duty to render the announcement of a deed true by executing it),[170] has no trouble understanding how an obligation can continue after death. But this does not tally with the fact that sometimes, especially after a long time has passed, we consider ourselves released from an obligation through death. My proposal lets us understand this. An obligation ordinarily does not disappear immediately on the death of the other person, because those with whom we have had valued mutual understandings do not immediately fall out of those understandings once they die.[171] But the obligation more or less rapidly loses force as the shared understanding of which it was a part also gradually fades away. We have a similar experience in drifting apart from people during life. For example, we feel that invitations telling others that they are welcome to visit lose force after a while if the understandings on which they were based fail to survive.

84. Our study of promising has not provided a basis for proving moral demands valid; rather, it has led us in the opposite direction; for not only did the concept of an obligation arising through promising prove to be unintelligible, but also understanding what it is that we do in promising did not require such a concept. Communicating an intention to someone, which is what so-called promising really amounts to, is part of the complex web of action and speech through which people learn about one another. What they learn will be important in determining their actions. Practically everything we do, we do in considering that certain things are true of certain other persons. In the determination of action, promises play a role in principle no different from that of anything else giving us knowledge about one another. That a promise was made is one consideration among many in determining action, a consideration not privileged by any overriding claim, but which may be supplemented, corrected, or even invalidated by the others. The matter becomes clearer if we consider, instead of the short-term promises treated in most of the literature, important long-term promises, such as marriage. What the promise of marriage means for one's actions is not that each partner henceforth can rightly demand certain things from the other and for his or her part falls under certain obligations. Its import for one's actions is just as great as that of a person's sincere declaration of intention to live together with someone faithfully.

In the sequel, not the promise but the sort of life fulfilling the promise will be what is important. At any rate, a person will be wise to act accordingly. To insist on the promise made by someone with whom living together has failed to lend that promise any reality would be empty legalism.

V. Autonomy

97. The *Groundwork*'s argument can be supplemented with the argument in §6 of the second *Critique*, although this argument rests on confusions.

98. The doctrine of the fact is irrelevant under the most natural interpretation because the facticity of the validity of the moral law makes a proof of this validity neither dispensable nor impossible.

99. The doctrine of the fact can also mean that no rational being can avoid knowing and taking into account the validity of the moral law. A proof of validity is then unnecessary.

100. The doctrine of the fact, so understood, is ad hoc and endangers moral agreement. The rational cannot be conceived as something that forces itself on us.

101. Following this idea, some people interpret the moral law as expressing pure practical reason. Such talk is unintelligible.

102. Kant's argument for the weakened principle of autonomy.

103. A further weakening.

104. Kant's talk of 'command conditionally' and 'unconditionally' in the argument is difficult to follow.

105. The distinction between hypothetical and categorical imperatives does not help here.

106. 'Command conditionally' and 'unconditionally' as indicating two ways of adopting the law stated in an imperative, namely, under the condition of one's own interest and not under this condition, respectively.

107. So interpreted, Kant's argument is not sound.

108. The autonomy principle can be justified by the fact that one can act only according to self-given laws.

109. Kant did not justify the autonomy principle this way. Yet he does hold that one can act only according to self-given laws.

110. Reasons for this doctrine are given by his analysis of action.

111. The argument is analytic, not empirical.

112. 'Acting according to laws' explained.

113. 'Acting according to laws' presents an alternative to conceiving action as the satisfaction of desire, and will as the faculty of desire.

114. That action should be understood as action according to laws follows from its intentionality.

115. Intentional action is the starting premise of the argument.

116. That action occurs only according to self-given laws is not refuted by cases usually described as actions according to a

prescription; for these cases can be explained as actions according to one's own law, in the choice of which the prescription was taken into account.

117. The inference from action only according to self-given laws to the autonomy principle.

118. The present conception of 'autonomy' is a formal conception.

119. Kant tightened up the autonomy principle by adding the words 'and yet universal.' The meaning of this phrase.

120. The required universal legislation must be softened to the condition that a moral law is capable of being agreed to by all rational beings.

121. The tightening up of the principle by the universality clause can be justified by the concept of a moral law.

122. The tightened principle of autonomy gives a necessary, but also a sufficient, condition for moral laws.

123. A procedure is thus found for proving the validity of moral laws.

124. Because moral laws are valid only through self-legislation, there are no valid moral demands. No moral law opposes one's own will.

125. The attempt to avoid this consequence by distinguishing a pure self from an empirical self. The shortcoming of this move.

126. Human will should be understood on the model of Kant's 'holy will': The 'ought' does not properly belong here.

127. Often it is difficult to decide whether something is demanded of someone by reason of his own will or for external reasons.

128. That a law would find agreement among all rational beings is no reason for adopting it. Moral laws are irrelevant.

85. The question of how a person can set up an obligation through certain actions by which he enters a contract or makes a promise (64) has not been answered. We simply do not understand how one can succeed in doing this. So demonstrating the validity of moral demands in this way is futile. But the other attempts at proving this have had just as little success. The result of my discussion so far is thus altogether negative; moral demands can be provided neither a justification nor a proof of their validity

(31). We have yet to consider the classical proposal for showing the validity of moral demands: Kant's idea of autonomy. It requires careful exposition because Kant presents it interwoven with the many strands of his view of moral philosophy, a view that itself developed over time, and both circumstances make understanding difficult. But it also deserves the most exact account, for it provides the boldest and ultimately most helpful answer to our question. Moreover, not only has it had a significant impact in the history of philosophy,[172] but also it is the starting point for independent attempts at practical philosophy and for historical reconstructions incorporating widely disparate viewpoints.[173] The following exegesis comes in three parts. The first (86–94) explains what is meant by 'autonomy' and uncovers a confusion, due to Kant, that has obfuscated the concept. The second (95–101) tests the most significant of Kant's attempts to confirm the validity of moral demands without employing the idea of autonomy. The third (102–128) lays out the argument for the principle of autonomy and draws some consequences for moral philosophy.

86. Kant introduces the concept of autonomy in the second chapter of the *Groundwork of the Metaphysics of Morals* (quoted in the following from Beck's translation, except the title, and referred to with "GMS" and the page number in Volume IV of the Academy edition):

> This principle I will call the principle of autonomy of the will in contrast to all other principles which I accordingly count under heteronomy. (GMS 433)

This statement shows that for Kant, there is only one principle of autonomy, but many principles of heteronomy;[174] for "this principle" *is* the principle of autonomy, whereas other principles are classified only as heteronomous. "This principle," which he intends to call the "principle of autonomy," is not stated by Kant at this point in the text. Still, one can hardly fail to identify it. It is the principle that at the beginning of the same paragraph Kant had accused his predecessors of having missed:

> Man was seen to be bound to laws by his duty, but it was not seen that he is subject only to his own, yet universal, legislation, and that he is only bound to act in accordance with his own will, which is, however, designed by nature to be a will giving universal laws. (GMS 432)

The second that-clause in this sentence, speaking of nature's purpose, creates added difficulty. To keep the main issue in view, I shall set aside this difficulty in the following and base my inquiry only on the first that-clause. The principle Kant has in mind is this: Man is subject only to his own and yet universal legislation. In the following, 'principle of autonomy' will mean this statement, until noted otherwise.

87. This interpretation agrees with the literal meaning of 'autonomy': 'self-lawfulness.' In Greek and early modern usage, the word denotes a political property, the ability of a state to make its own laws and to act independently.[175] Kant was the first to extend the concept to individual agents. The older, political usage meanwhile remained familiar to him.[176] 'Autonomy' thus characteristically contrasts with 'autocracy,' also political in origin, which Kant introduced in the lectures on ethics:

> The power which the soul has over all faculties and over the whole condition, i.e., the power to subject this condition, without compulsion, to its own free choice, is an autocracy.[177]

Autocracy, literally 'self-rule,' is a relation of power. Autonomy obtains, if I am subject, not to the power that I employ against myself but to the law that I give myself.[178] Autonomy is distinguished from autocracy as Rousseau's republic, the law-governed state,[179] is distinguished from despotism.[180] Whereas Plato's moral philosophy has been called aristocratic, Kant's theory of autonomy is an attempt at republicanism in moral philosophy.

88. The idea of universal legislation appears in still another context in Kant, however, and a clarification of the difference is important in understanding 'autonomy.' In the paragraph of the *Groundwork* preceding the sentence just quoted, he states that

> . . . if there is a categorical imperative (a law for the will of every rational being), it can only command that everything be done from the maxim of its will as one which could have as its object only itself considered as giving universal laws. (GMS 432)

Or, in the simpler version he uses somewhat later, we are commanded

> . . . to act only so that the will through its maxims could regard itself at the same time as universally lawgiving. (GMS 434)[181]

Like the principle of autonomy, this command involves the idea of one's "own, yet universal, legislation." For maxims are rules that one sets for one's own acting,[182] and hence the result of one's own legislation. And if the will, in adopting a maxim, can thereby at the same time regard itself as making universal law, then the maxim fulfills the condition of one's "own, yet universal, legislation."

89. The command of the categorical imperative and the principle of autonomy differ in what function they ascribe to the idea of one's own and yet universal legislation. In the categorical imperative, the concept of one's own and yet universal legislation constitutes a criterion for actions. Some actions will satisfy the condition of following from a maxim by means of which the will can at the same time regard itself as making universal law. Other actions will not satisfy it. The categorical imperative requires that only actions of the first kind be done. By contrast, in the principle of autonomy the concept of one's own and yet universal legislation is a criterion for laws of action. Some laws for action will satisfy the condition of originating in one's own and yet universal legislation, whereas other laws will not; and the principle of autonomy says that only laws of the first kind are valid moral laws. Hence, the distinction does not rest on the fact that the categorical imperative is used to make a command whereas the principle of autonomy is used to make a statement. The distinction holds even if we replace the command with a statement of its validity, so that we now have statement opposing statement. The statement might run as follows: Human beings are subject to the command to do only those actions through whose maxims the will can regard itself as making universal law. In contrast, the principle of autonomy says the following: Human beings are subject only to laws deriving from their own and yet universal legislation. But these are two different things. The first statement asserts the validity of a moral command; the second asserts that there is a certain condition for the validity of moral commands. The difference remains even if we add to the autonomy principle the statement that human beings are in fact subject to at least one command originating in their own and yet universal legislation. This still is not to say that human beings are subject to the command to do only those actions through whose maxims the will can regard itself as making law. To be sure, it may be that this command (i.e., the categorical imperative) does satisfy the condition stated in the principle of autonomy. Perhaps, even, it is the only command satisfying the condition, and perhaps the supplementary assumption just mentioned holds for it, namely, that human beings actually are subject to it. In this case to act only according to maxims by means of which the will can regard itself as making universal law would be a valid, and indeed uniquely valid, command for human beings, originating in their own universal legislation. But this is not obviously so; it still needs to be shown. Should it turn out, however, as is equally possible, that the categorical imperative does not satisfy the condition established by the autonomy principle, then the two statements will turn out to be incompatible.

90. Kant confuses the principle of autonomy with the command of the categorical imperative. Thus, he writes under the heading "The Autonomy of the Will as the Supreme Principle of Morality":

> Autonomy of the will is that property of it by which it is a law to itself independent of any property of objects of volition. Hence the principle of autonomy

is: Never choose except in such a way that the maxims of the choice are comprehended in the same volition as a universal law. (GMS 440)

In the first sentence here, we recognize the principle of autonomy: A law for the human will is that will itself, and, one might add, only that will. The second sentence states the command to act only under the condition of a possible universal legislation through the maxims.[183] Kant's transition from the first to the second sentence, without any further argument, with only a "hence," is unwarranted and attests the confusion. He accordingly uses the word 'autonomy' in two senses. Besides the meaning determined by the autonomy principle, the word often denotes an action's property of arising from a maxim that can serve as universal law. Thus at one point Kant says that morality is

. . . the relation of actions to the autonomy of the will, i.e., to possible universal lawgiving by maxims of the will. (GMS 439)

Or he says that the principle of morality

. . . must be a categorical imperative and that the imperative commands neither more nor less than this very autonomy. (GMS 440)

'Autonomy' thus alternates between denoting something that itself is morally commanded and denoting a condition under which alone something can be valid as a moral demand. The confusion becomes apparent toward the end of the second chapter of the *Groundwork,* where Kant describes the autonomy of the good will as follows:

. . . the capability of the maxims of every good will to make themselves universal laws is itself the sole law which the will of every rational being imposes on itself. (GMS 444)

No reason is to be seen why the will of every rational being that subjects itself to laws therefore imposes on itself as the sole law the fitness of its maxims for universal law.

Either this is a trivial law that the will cannot but fulfill (because every law that it gives itself must be such that it can give it to itself), or it is a law that imposes substantial restrictions, and then the will giving itself this law will not be justified by the will being subject only to universal laws that it gives itself.

91. This confusion also explains an inconsistency in the way Kant introduces the autonomy principle (86). There is only one principle of autonomy, it was said, but many principles of heteronomy. But if the principle of autonomy is just the statement 'man is subject only to his own and yet universal legislation,' then similarly there can be only one principle of heteronomy, namely, the negation of this statement. So when Kant is speaking of many principles of heteronomy, he cannot be taken to mean by such a principle a statement about the conditions for valid moral laws. He must mean a moral law itself or the corresponding statement that a certain moral law is valid. Thus, principles of heteronomy will be laws requiring actions that are not always actions in accordance with maxims through which the will can regard itself as making universal law. That there are many such laws is obvious. The counterpart of principles of heteronomy in this sense is likewise a moral law or the statement that a certain moral law is valid, not a statement about the conditions for valid moral laws. It is that law (or statement of its validity) that requires acting only from maxims through which the will can regard itself as making universal law; that is, it is the law stated in the categorical imperative. A single principle of autonomy is being opposed to the many principles of heteronomy only because the former has been mistaken for the categorical imperative.

92. One understands how the confusion can arise. Two levels of reflection are mixed up. The categorical imperative uses the criterion of the lawlikeness of maxims to select certain actions as morally demanded. The principle of autonomy, on the other hand, uses the criterion of one's own and yet universal legislation to select from commands aimed at actions those that are valid. The categorical imperative says something about what a person ought to do.

The principle of autonomy says something about what can rightly be said about what a person ought to do. The condition imposed on possible moral demands may indeed be so strict that only one such demand satisfies it, and this demand may turn out to be the categorical imperative. But this would have to be specifically shown. Kant gives no such argument. Misled by the confusion, he does not even see the necessity for such an argument, and, as the passages quoted show, he simply takes the two principles to be equivalent. The confusion remains unnoticed because Kant uses a series of correspondingly ambiguous terms. Thus, "the autonomy of the will as the supreme principle of morality" (GMS 440) can mean either that autonomy is the highest moral command or that it is the condition for any valid command. Similarly, talk of "the idea of the will of every rational being as making universal law" (GMS 431; similarly GMS 432) does not tell us whether actions or demands for actions are to be judged according to this idea. Accordingly, the term 'idea' can be read two ways here. It can refer to a representation that, though not true, is useful for orienting ourselves. But it can also refer to a principle that must be true. The first sense obtains when autonomy is identified with what is commanded by the categorical imperative. The imperative can then be this: Act as if your will were making universal law. Actually, Kant did on occasion use this 'as if' in formulating the categorical imperative.[184] The 'as if' announces an 'idea' in the first sense. If autonomy is seen as the condition on valid moral imperatives, however, the second sense of 'idea' obtains. The will then actually makes universal law and is subject only to this law. Once again, the ambiguity can be located in Kant's saying that the will "must be regarded also as self-legislative and only for this reason as being subject to the law (of which it can regard itself as the author)" (GMS 431). The formulation does not determine whether the will must be regarded as self-legislating and can regard itself as the originator of the law because it is in fact self-legislating and is in fact the originator of the law or because the fiction that this is so is especially suitable for determining what is morally demanded.

93. One could try in the following way to defend Kant against the charge that he confused the autonomy principle and the categorical imperative: According to Kant, not every human will but only the rational will is subject to its own universal legislation; autonomy applies to the will not as determinable but as determined by reason. A rationally determined will, however, is simply a will whose actions correspond to the law expressed by the categorical imperative – a will, that is, acting according to maxims fit for universal law. The principle of autonomy and the categorical imperative are thus actually equivalent in the sense that the former applies only as far as the latter is obeyed. That is to say, a person is subject only to her own universal legislation just in case she acts only from maxims fit for universal law. So on this account, Kant can rightly say that the fitness of its maxims for universal law is the only law that a will, subject only to its own legislation, imposes on itself (90). It may be true that the principle of autonomy lays down a condition for valid moral imperatives whereas the categorical imperative is itself a moral imperative; but, practically speaking, this is irrelevant because this condition for valid moral imperatives is in force only where this moral imperative is obeyed. But, first of all, Kant's text does not support this reading. As the passage quoted earlier (86) shows, it is man, not merely a rational human will, who is subject only to his own and yet universal legislation. Second, it can be said against this proposal that it renders the autonomy principle irrelevant, whereas for Kant, according to the passage quoted earlier, recognition of the principle meant the decisive step beyond his predecessors in moral philosophy. It is irrelevant to say that a will, determined from the outset as rational, in acting rationally follows only its own universal legislation. It is superfluous for this will expressly to give itself the law that is fixed as the law of its actions anyway. Granting autonomy to a will becomes an empty phrase, if through presupposition one already assures oneself of the law which that will alone can give itself. 'Good children may do as they please' says nothing more than 'Children, be good!' The principle that the rational will is subject only to its own universal legislation might be expected to aid in demonstrating that this law of rational action is simply the one expressed in the categorical imperative. But this hope too is deceptive, for here again the distinction between a moral imperative and the condition for the validity of moral imperatives comes into play. That the rational will is subject only to its own law, the law of reason, is no ground for assuming that this law consists in the fitness of its maxims to be law. For that assumption, other reasons must be adduced. To be sure, sometimes this does seem to have been Kant's idea; a rational will, obeying only itself, can set itself as a principle only that of rationality (i.e., the fitness of its maxims to be law). But again, this simply presupposes what was to be shown, namely, that the rationality of action consists in the fitness of maxims to be universal law.

94. We have been seeking a proof of the validity of moral demands. The distinction between the categorical imperative and the principle of autonomy, or the corresponding distinction between the two meanings that 'autonomy' takes in Kant's usage, is important in this regard because it clarifies the difference between two kinds of such proof offered by Kant. Suppose that the categorical imperative does not fulfill the condition imposed by the autonomy principle on moral demands and that for this reason the autonomy principle is dropped. Then it will be the categorical imperative that is in the predicament we have been discussing, namely, that of needing a proof of its validity or, as Kant says, a proof "that that kind of imperative really exists" (*"dass ein solcher Imperativ wirklich stattfinde"*) (GMS 425). To this end, Kant has brought forth two considerations, the argument from the third chapter of the *Groundwork* and the doctrine of the fact of reason from the *Critique of Practical Reason*. But suppose that in case of conflict the autonomy principle takes precedence over the categorical imperative, which is then acknowledged as invalid, or suppose that no conflict arises and the categorical imperative fulfills the condition of autonomy. Then a proof of the validity of moral demands by means of the idea of autonomy can be attempted. It is true that in Kant's presentation the argument from autonomy, which does not employ the categorical imperative, is less prominent than the first two considerations, which make no use of the autonomy principle. Yet the actual strength of the arguments is just the reverse. The third chapter of the *Groundwork* offers no hope of a satisfactory proof of the validity of moral demands, and the doctrine of the fact of reason does just as little to remove doubts on this point (i.e., about the validity of moral demands). Only the idea of autonomy offers prospects of such a proof and hence the prospects of moving a step beyond the entirely negative results obtained thus far. In the following, I shall pursue these prospects in detail. First (95–101), though, I must state the reasons for distrusting the considerations by means of which Kant himself meant to safeguard the validity of moral demands.

95. That the argument in the third chapter of the *Groundwork* does not fall back on the principle of autonomy may seem an odd claim. But the impression that matters stand otherwise comes from Kant's confusion and the resulting ambiguity of 'autonomy.' Kant starts from the idea that the autonomy principle applies to a free will (i.e., that a free will is subject only to self-given laws). As a result of the confusion, however, he thinks himself justified in assuming that a free will is subject to the law of acting "according to no other maxim than that which can also have itself as a universal law for its object. And this is just the formula of the categorical imperative and the principle of morality. Therefore a free will and a will under moral laws are identical" (GMS 447). The argument in the third chapter of the *Groundwork* for the validity of the categorical imperative is based on this proposition, namely, that a free will is subject to the demand expressed in the categorical imperative. The argument uses the principle of autonomy – a free will is subject only to self-given laws – only to derive this proposition. But because the purported derivation consists only in replacing this meaning of 'autonomy' with another, it is no exaggeration to say that the autonomy principle does not enter the argument of the third chapter. Already, the statement that we recognize ourselves as "subject to the autonomy of the will" (GMS 434) shows that autonomy in the sense given by the principle of autonomy is not in question here. To this autonomy one cannot be subject, because it is rather the condition for one's being subject to any law. In fact, 'autonomy' here refers to what is demanded in the categorical imperative.

96. The argumentation in the third chapter of the *Groundwork* is not promising, for the reason that it cannot dispense with the proposition that a free will is the same thing as a will under moral laws, while offering no justification that would go beyond confusing the two meanings of 'autonomy.' Kant first considers (GMS 447f.) that a rational being having a will cannot act except under the idea of freedom and so is actually free in a practical respect. Thus, Kant can set aside theoretical doubts about human freedom,[185] but then he has advanced the desired proof for the validity of moral demands only if it is also true that a free will is a will under moral laws. Indeed, he falls back on this proposition when he writes, "All laws which are inseparably bound up with freedom hold" (GMS 448) for a rational being who has a will. With this, the argument would have reached its goal, but the premise is unwarranted. In what follows, Kant himself seems to have lost faith in the argument. To be sure, the question "But why should I subject myself to this principle?" (GMS 449) (i.e., the moral principle expressed in the categorical imperative) can hardly be answered satisfactorily by a consideration that assumes no more than the concept of a rational being endowed with a will. Kant meanwhile seeks the argument's weak point in the wrong place. He criticizes the claim that in practice humans are to be regarded as free on grounds that it already presupposes the validity of the moral law and thus makes the argument circular. But his charge is unwarranted. The first consideration just noted, according to which a rational being having a will is, in practical respects, also free, does not presuppose any moral law to which that being is subject.[186] To rectify what he mistakes for a weakness, Kant in a second consideration (GMS 450–455) summons the doctrine of two worlds, one of sensibility and the other of understanding. The defensibility and even the intelligibility of this doctrine need not be pursued here. Even assuming that it would help us to establish human freedom, an argument on this basis for the validity of moral demands still requires the premise that a free will is a will under moral laws, and Kant unmistakably appeals to this premise. But it is both unfounded and incredible,[187] and the two-worlds doctrine has no import for the argument as long as it fails to make this premise dispensable.[188] So the proof here breaks down at just the point it did in the first consideration.

97. One could try to save the proof by falling back on the *Critique of Practical Reason*. The problematic proposition that a free will is a will standing under moral laws is proved, one could say, in §6 of that work,[189] and proved without confusing the two meanings of 'autonomy.' To be sure, in the later work, Kant makes no further use of the proposition but, on the contrary, infers human freedom from the fact of the moral law. This, however, should not prevent one from supplementing the *Groundwork*'s argument with the proof of §6. But again, this hope is illusory. In the first place, even in the best case, §6 proves less than what was meant to be proved through the confusion of the two meanings of 'autonomy,' less too than the argument of the *Groundwork* requires. It would have to be shown that a free will is indeed subject to the moral demand expressed by the categorical imperative. But §6 claims to prove only that the moral demand expressed by the categorical imperative is alone suitable to necessarily determine a free will. But that only a categorical imperative can be valid for a free will does not yet mean that this imperative is actually valid. This does not impair the argument in the *Critique,* because the validity of the categorical imperative, not secured with this argument, will be established through the fact of reason. But the *Groundwork*'s argument cannot get along with just the weaker premise. In the second place, the proof in §6 actually does not achieve its stated goal. The argument is as follows:

> Since the material of the practical law, i.e., an object of the maxim, cannot be given except empirically,

and since a free will must be independent of all empirical conditions (i.e., those belonging to the world
of sense) and yet be determinable, a free will must
find its ground of determination in the law, but independently of the material of the law. But besides the
latter there is nothing in a law except the legislative
form. Therefore, the legislative form, in so far as it is
contained in the maxim, is the only thing which can
constitute a determining ground of the will. (Academy edition, V, p. 29; quoted here and in the following from Beck's translation)

Two objections may be raised. On the one hand, the argument trades on a double meaning of "independent of all
empirical conditions." Granted that a free will does not
depend on empirical conditions in the sense that no em-
pirically determinable state or process effects a determination of will, and granted, therefore, that a free will is not
subject to the causality of nature, we still cannot claim that
a free will is not determinable by considerations of circumstances of which experience alone gives knowledge.
Hence, if by 'determining ground' of the will we are to
understand the consideration determining the will, it does
not follow from the freedom of the will that the material
of the law cannot be a determining ground for it. By 'determining ground' of the will, however, we must understand the consideration determining the will, for it is absurd to suppose that the legislative form of the maxims,
which form Kant identifies as the determining ground of a
free will, should not be a determining consideration rather
than, say, an influence.[190] On the other hand, 'legislative
form' has two senses. That a law has only material and
legislative form presumably means that only two kinds of
statements can be made about a law. We give the material
of the law by stating what sort of action the law prescribes.
We speak of the form of the law in characterizing it as a
law. But it is absurd to make legislative form in this sense a
determining ground of the will, for something is a determining ground of the will in determining the will to act or

to act in a certain way. But the property of being a law does not distinguish one kind of action from another, for the reason that this property cannot be meaningfully ascribed to actions. Rather, the property of being a law singles out one class of determinations of actions, as opposed to, say, advice or commands. But it makes no sense to say that the will should be determined not by what determines action but by something that is only a property of some determinations of actions, such as being a law. We could just as well say that all candidates on the list having rejected our offer, we should now appoint the list itself. There is a second sense in which Kant speaks of a legislative form that is to be the determining ground of the will. In this sense, it is that form of the maxims "through which they are fitted for being universal laws,"[191] in other words, the common property of those maxims that meet the criterion established by the categorical imperative. This must be what is meant, for only then does the passage I quoted offer an argument from freedom to the moral law, an argument needed for the immediately following claim: "Thus freedom and unconditional practical law reciprocally imply each other." To make legislative form in this new sense the determining ground of the will is certainly not absurd. Unlike the first sense, it does delineate a class of actions, those in accordance with a maxim that can hold as universal law. But to make legislative form in this sense the determining ground of the will is unwarranted; for in the foregoing argument, 'legislative form' meant something else. The confusion of the two meanings is similar to that for 'autonomy.' In both cases, two levels of reflection have not been kept apart, so that determinations of actions are confused with the characteristics of determinations of actions.

98. The *Critique of Practical Reason* responds to the question, How can the validity of moral demands be proved? with the doctrine of the fact of reason. It responds to this question not by providing the requested proof but by trying to show the proof to be impossible. The doctrine of the fact is most succinctly stated in the section entitled "Of the Deduction of the Principles of Pure Practical Reason":

> Moreover, the moral law is given, as an apodictically
> certain fact, as it were, of pure reason, a fact of which
> we are a priori conscious, even if it be granted that no
> example could be found in which it has been followed
> exactly. Thus the objective reality of the moral law
> can be proved through no deduction, through no ex-
> ertion of the theoretical, speculative, or empirically
> supported reason; and, even if one were willing to
> renounce its apodictic certainty, it could not be con-
> firmed by any experience and thus proved a posteri-
> ori. Nevertheless, it is firmly established of itself.[192]

The doctrine of the fact of reason has been attacked and
defended on various grounds.[193] Interpreted in one natural
way, however, the doctrine is irrelevant to proving the
validity of the moral law. But such a proof Kant, too,
intends to give, for by "objective reality of the moral law"
he evidently means what a bit earlier in the text was called
"its objective and universal validity."[194] The doctrine is
irrelevant because even if the moral law, or better, perhaps, the validity of the moral law, is a fact of pure reason,
it does not follow that its validity cannot be proved in any
way and yet is firmly established. To say of something
that it is a fact is not also to say that it cannot be proved. If,
for example, someone says, "It is a fact that the West
German constitution was proclaimed on May 23, 1949,"
then he has not exempted himself from showing that the
matter does stand this way and that this is a fact. Still less
has he declared that showing this is impossible.[195] So even
if the law or its validity is a fact in a sense to be determined
more exactly, this does not affect the demand for a proof
of its validity. Thus, the second *Critique* does not counter
this demand with an argument based on the facticity of the
moral law and showing it to be valid, yet not demonstra-
bly so; it counters with the blunt claim that this is how
matters stand. Doubt about the validity of moral demands, a doubt that at least the *Groundwork* does not find
absurd,[196] has not been dispelled.

99. One might object that this reading neglects what is

most important about the statements I have quoted. They do not say that either the moral law or its validity is a fact of reason, but that the moral law is, as it were, given as a fact of pure reason. But it is not quite clear what it means for something to be given as a fact of pure reason. It obviously means to be known in some particular way, but the question is, What way? A plausible answer is found if one recalls how the word 'fact' is used in connection with deliberation about action. Here, 'fact' denotes not only what is so but also what, in addition, practical deliberation must presently take into account, that from which the deliberation must proceed and which must not be neglected if deliberation is not to go astray. In a practical sense, facts are what cannot be avoided, what we cannot rationally forgo taking into account. That the moral law is given as a fact accordingly means that one is cognizant of it in such a way that in all practical considerations one knows of its validity and has to take this validity into account. And that it is given as a fact of pure reason means that every rational being is cognizant of it in this way. Whoever makes use of reason, so the doctrine goes, is cognizant of the validity of the moral law and must attend to this validity. To use Kant's eloquent metaphor, the moral law "forces itself upon us."[197] Its facticity consists in this 'forcing itself.' From the doctrine of the fact of reason, so interpreted, it still does not follow that the validity of the moral law is impossible to prove. But it does follow that it is unnecessary to prove this. What was supposed to be proved forces itself upon us anyway. Our doubts about the validity of moral demands can in this way be silenced.

100. But so construed, the doctrine of fact is implausible. It is an ad hoc solution, one that secures a seemingly indispensable premise by means of a doctrine introduced only to this end. Henrich has shown that only after failing in the attempt to prove the validity of the moral law did Kant turn to the doctrine of the fact of reason.[198] For this reason, Henrich sees in the doctrine Kant's "latest and most mature answer to the problem of the absoluteness of the good."[199] Just this circumstance, however, may be taken as evidence for the ad hoc character of the doctrine of the fact. Considering that so far Kant had constructed his moral philosophy so as to culminate in a proof for the validity of moral demands, a goal still evident in the *Groundwork*,[200] his transition to the doctrine of the fact might rather be described by saying, borrowing from Russell, that Kant, when he could no longer get on with honest toil, had recourse to theft.[201] But above all, the doctrine of the fact of reason, so understood, is unconvincing in the matter at hand. It raises, without justification, an extraordinarily far-reaching claim: Everyone knows that the moral law is valid. And rather than defend this validity against criticism, it simply cuts off criticism. It does not present those who are skeptical of the validity of the moral law with convincing reasons that would dispel this doubt, but charges them with insincerity, because, after all, they cannot avoid knowing what they claim to doubt. It thereby endangers discussion of morality and moral philosophy. Whoever is told, in response to her expressed doubts, that she cannot mean what she says has good reason to break off discussion. To be sure, both considerations, the historical as well as the material, do not speak conclusively against the doctrine of the fact. What makes it unacceptable and sets off the polemic against it is something else. The determination of what is right to do cannot be something whose claim on us simply ineluctably confronts us. The rational cannot be the sort of thing that forces itself upon us. We must grasp it as our own and be able to recognize ourselves in it. This conviction is what guided Hegel in his attack on "cold duty," that "undigested lump in the stomach."[202] Modifying the way Hegel spoke (in the *Phenomenology*) of the absolute, one could say this of the good: If it were to be brought any closer to us through the demand, it presumably would deride this cunning, if it were not by itself already with us and so wanted to be; or we would deride it.[203] To be sure, it still is not clear what it means to grasp the rational not as 'forcing itself upon us' but as our own. Besides, this is a mere conviction; so far, it is no more justified than the doctrine of fact. But one way to interpret this idea has already been mentioned: the principle of autonomy. Determining what is right to do in accordance with this principle would satisfy that conviction.

101. It will be objected that although the autonomy principle does satisfy the conviction that the determination of the good must be our own, the same end can be attained by a weaker claim. Such a claim can be found in Kant's reflection on whether an unconditional law is "merely the self-consciousness of a pure practical reason."[204] On this suggestion, one recognizes in the moral law simply the expression of pure practical reason. This is how Beck interprets Kant,[205] and indeed it is a prevalent reading. The command of the categorical imperative, so the interpretation goes, originates in the capacity of human reason by itself to determine the will, and the command expresses only this 'autonomy.'[206] 'Autonomy,' however, seems to have a new meaning here compared with those used earlier (90), and this meaning is not wholly clear. It is not clear what 'pure practical reason' is and what is meant by saying that reason by itself is able to determine the will.[207] But suppose this can be adequately explained. It still is unintelligible to say that the moral law has its origin in pure practical reason or is the expression of the latter. A sentence expresses its meaning, and a gesture expresses a feeling or originates in it; but I do not understand what it means to say that an ability belonging to human beings – reason, or, in particular, pure practical reason – generates a law for their actions, or is expressed by such a law. At best it can be said of an ability that it is expressed in one's performance, or that it generates performance. Accordingly, we would have an expression of reason whenever someone deliberated or acted rationally. But I do not understand how a law for that person's actions or the fact of the law's validity can be an expression of reason or stem from reason.[208] It is not simply that nothing speaks for the assumption; I do not understand what it means to say that what one ought to do is an expression of what one can do. Nevertheless, talk of the expression of reason is common in the literature.[209] One may understand that talk as meaning that he must lay down the moral law who is subject to it; that is to say, a moral law must satisfy the autonomy principle. But this takes us back to the possibility set aside earlier (94), namely, of proving the validity of a moral demand that satisfies the autonomy condition by just this fact, that is, proving its validity by arguing that it derives from one's own and yet universal legislation. Of Kant's other proposals for securing its validity, there remains only the doctrine of the fact of reason under the strong interpretation, and it seems unacceptable for the reason given. There is no argument using weaker premises that would dispel doubt about the validity of moral demands. Fact or autonomy, there is no third way.

102. Kant gives an argument for the autonomy principle. Here is the text between the two sentences quoted earlier (86) that introduced the principle:

> For if one thought of him as subject only to a law (whatever it may be), this necessarily implied some interest as a stimulus or compulsion to obedience because the law did not arise from his will. Rather, his will was constrained by something else according to a law to act in a certain way. By this strictly necessary consequence, however, all the labor of finding a supreme ground for duty was irrevocably lost, and one never arrived at duty but only at the necessity of action from a certain interest. This might be his own interest or that of another, but in either case the imperative always had to be conditional and could not at all serve as a moral command. (GMS 432f.)

More precisely, this is an argument not for the autonomy principle itself but for a statement twice weakened in comparison. The first weakening consists in striking 'and yet universal' from the original version, turning the sentence into this: Man is subject only to his own legislation. That the argument does not attempt to prove more than this is evident from the fact that it considers only the alternative to this, namely, that the law does not spring from one's own will and that the will is necessitated by something else in conformity to law.[210] From now on, accordingly, and contrary to how the term has been used thus far (86), 'principle of autonomy' will refer to this statement, namely, that man is subject only to his own legislation. I shall come back to the original version later (119–122).

103. The principle of autonomy is easy to understand.

'Man' is tantamount to 'every man,' 'subject to his own legislation' is short for 'subject to laws stemming from his legislation,' and someone is 'subject' to a law if and only if it is valid for him – 'valid' in the sense explained earlier (30), so that the person in question ought to follow the law. The principle of autonomy says, then: For every man, only those laws are valid that spring from his own legislation. More briefly: Only self-given laws are valid. In the following, I shall also call laws not stemming from legislation by the person they address 'prescriptions.' The principle of autonomy negatively says, then, There are no valid prescriptions. This includes the statement that there are no valid moral prescriptions. It is only the latter claim that the argument just quoted (102) was intended to validate, and this brings about the second weakening of the original thesis. The weaker proposition could also be put as follows: In moral matters, man is subject only to his own legislation, as opposed to this: Man is nowhere subject to anything but his own legislation. That the argument aims at proving only the weaker claim is evident from its conclusion. The result stated there is merely that a law not stemming from one's own legislation cannot serve as a moral law; whether it can serve as any other kind of valid law remains an open question.

104. The argument I quoted for the autonomy principle is not so easy to understand. It has this form: Valid moral laws spring from one's own legislation, for a valid moral law commands unconditionally, but laws not proceeding from one's own legislation command only conditionally. What is difficult to understand is the meanings of 'command conditionally' and 'unconditionally.'

105. It is natural here to appeal to Kant's distinction between hypothetical and categorical imperatives. The argument then runs as follows: Valid moral laws stem from one's own legislation, for a valid moral law can be expressed only in a categorical imperative, but laws not stemming from one's own legislation can be expressed only in hypothetical imperatives. This version of the argument is favored by its closeness to the text. Kant states explicitly (GMS 425) that a moral law can be expressed only in a categorical imperative, and the second premise seems to reflect his view as well (GMS 444). But, actually, this version is unsatisfactory. The distinction between categorical and hypothetical imperatives proves unintelligible on closer scrutiny, and Kant has not managed to pin it down with some criterion. Hypothetical and categorical imperatives can indeed be distinguished formally, according to whether or not a conditional clause is attached to the imperatival main clause. But this is not the distinction Kant had in mind and that required by his program.[211] Thus, it would be implausible in the present case to classify prescriptions and valid moral laws under hypothetical and categorical imperatives formally distinguished this way. It simply is not true that prescriptions always come with, and valid moral laws always come without, a conditional clause attached to the imperative. But Kant failed to provide any distinction other than this formal one.[212] So the argument for the autonomy principle cannot be reconstructed by using the distinction between categorical and hypothetical imperatives.

106. That a prescription "necessarily [implies] some interest as a stimulus or compulsion" puts us on another track, for one may wonder why such an interest should be necessary for a prescription, but not for a self-legislated law. The answer, presumably, is that only such an interest provides the person addressed by the prescription with a good reason for acting in accordance with it, whereas a person already has reason enough to act in accordance with her own, self-legislated law even without such an interest. A person who did not have sufficient reason to follow a law also would not have needed to give it to herself in the first place. But in this view, a person has no reason to do what is prescribed so long as there is not some interest added. That an interest 'stimulates or compels' probably should be understood to mean that one always has an interest in carrying out a prescription when the prescribed action itself seems attractive or when the person prescribing it makes it attractive by offering the reliable prospect of a reward or when that person compels with the prospect of punishment in case of omission. If one then says that such an added interest makes the imperative 'always conditional,' whereas the moral imperative is 'unconditional,' then this is a distinction not of two kinds of imperatives but of two ways of adopting as one's own the law expressed in the imperative. That a prescription commands conditionally would then mean that the person on whom the prescription is imposed adopts a corresponding rule of action, if at all, only conditionally. She adopts as a rule a conditional statement whose consequent alone specifies the prescribed way of acting, but whose antecedent specifies some interest she may have. Suppose that truthfulness is prescribed to someone, and prescribed in the form of a categorical command. The rule that she sets herself for her actions, if she wants to comply with the prescription, could be this: Whenever I want to keep the favor of the person who has issued the prescription, then I will be truthful. Or this: Whenever I want to support trust among people, I will be truthful. If this trust or favor means nothing to her, she has no reason to be truthful, whereas she has a reason if it means something to her. On the other hand, that a moral imperative commands unconditionally will mean that whoever wants to follow the relevant moral law will adopt a rule of action not containing any such condition of self-interest. Such a person then adopts the rule of total truthfulness or truthfulness toward certain individuals or under certain conditions, but not truthfulness under the condition of having a certain aim. But she will adopt a rule not involving any condition of self-interest because she has grounds for being truthful independently of what her interest may be. On this account, the argument for moral laws being self-legislative may be stated as follows: One has grounds for acting according to a prescription only if one pursues a certain aim; one has grounds for acting according to a moral law no matter what one's aims are; hence, moral laws are not prescriptions. This does not mean, of course, that someone who follows a moral law actually does not have aims when acting. The claim is that someone who follows a moral law has grounds for doing so independent of whether or not she has a certain aim, whereas one who follows a prescription does not have any such independent grounds.

107. Perhaps this view of the matter comes close to what Kant had in mind with his doctrine of categorical and hypothetical imperatives. It would then be wrong to describe it as a doctrine of two kinds of imperatives or of two ways of commanding. We should rather read Kant as distinguishing two sorts of grounds for following a law: those depending on one's own interest and those not depending on it. Yet this reconstruction is also unsatisfactory in the matter at hand. The argument is intelligible, but not sound, for one of the premises is doubtful. Not doubtful is the premise that in following a moral law one has grounds for this independent of one's interest; this may indeed lie in the concept of moral law (10). Doubtful is the premise that one has grounds for acting according to a prescription only if one pursues a particular aim. A person could claim that her grounds for obeying some prescriptions no more depend on her interests than do the grounds for acting according to moral laws. These are purely objective grounds, she might hold, and ulterior motives, such as gaining the favor of whoever issued the prescription, are mere imputations. To be sure, it is doubtful that there is any such 'noble' obedience. But it cannot be ruled out without further argument. As long as it is not ruled out, the reconstructed argument does not prevail.

108. Yet there is a justification for the principle of autonomy: Only self-legislated laws are valid, because one can act only according to self-legislated laws. This is a justification not only for the proposition that is weaker compared with the autonomy principle, namely, that in moral matters a person is subject only to her own legislation (103). It is also a justification for the autonomy principle itself: A person is always subject to her own legislation alone. She is subject to it alone because one cannot act according to an alien law. Laws cannot be 'taken up' into one's will.[213] There is no receptivity of practical reason. One always acts according to one's own laws.

109. Kant did not justify the autonomy principle in this way. In any event, the passage I have been discussing (102) can hardly be understood along these lines. But Kant could have justified it this way: His doctrine does hold that one can act only according to self-legislated laws. He calls self-given laws of action 'maxims.' More precisely, one should say that maxims form a subset of the self-given laws, but their specific difference of greater scope need not concern us here.[214] So the proposed ground for the autonomy principle is this: One can act only according to maxims. That Kant believed this is clear, because the categorical imperative determines the morality of actions according to the maxims on which they are based. Because all action is supposed to fall under the claim of moral law expressed in the categorical imperative, all actions must follow maxims.

110. Reasons for saying that one always acts according to one's own law can be found in Kant's analysis of action:

> Everything in nature works according to laws. Only a rational being has the capacity of acting according to the conception of laws, i.e., according to principles. This capacity is will. Since reason is required for the derivation of actions from laws, will is nothing else than practical reason. (GMS 412)[215]

This passage does not explicitly mention maxims or self-given laws. But as I argued in more detail elsewhere, that is what the principles mentioned here are.[216] They are not moral principles,[217] for otherwise the definition would not cover the will in general, but only the will as obeying moral law. The passage, however, attempts to isolate what is characteristic about any effect of will as compared with effects of nature. Now, effects of nature come about in ways governed by law; that is, they can be correctly described by lawlike statements. Actions may also be law-governed, for the rational being who acts is no less a thing of nature. At least the passage does not rule this out. Yet whether or not actions manifest lawfulness in this sense, as opposed to natural effects, they are performed by a being who in acting follows a law. Departing from how words are used in the sentences quoted, we may express their content thus: Natural effects are subject to laws, whereas we act according to laws. In order to act according to a law, however, the agent must have an idea of it. An object of nature as such does not know the law describing its behavior. Only beings can act, then, who are capable of having general ideas and of subsuming individual cases under them. Only rational beings can act. But for a being to act according to a law, it does not suffice that the being have an idea of the law and moreover produce effects that as a matter of fact instantiate the law; for then the law-fulness of the effects could still be produced behind that being's back, as it were – not without its own activity, to be sure, but without its will. For example, I may have an idea of what it would be like to become an alcoholic, and step by step I may actually become one, without, how-ever, willing that law to govern my behavior. To act ac-cording to a law, I not only must represent to myself how it could be a law of my action but also must will that it be a law of my action. That is to say, I must make it a law of my action. Laws that are laws of my action in the sense of correctly describing it can hold without my knowledge and will. Laws that are laws of my action in the sense that I act according to them do not hold independent of my knowledge and will. I make them valid in willing that they be laws of my action in the sense of their correctly describ-ing it. Because the law according to which I act owes its validity to my willing it to be the law correctly describing my action, it is a self-given law. And because action is defined as action according to laws, we may say that one can act only according to self-given laws.[218]

111. The argument makes an analytic, not empirical, claim. It is not that there simply are no actions not done according to a self-given law. The claim is that this prop-erty – being performed according to a self-given law – belongs to our concept of an action, or it is being proposed that actions be thought of this way. Whether assertion or proposal, a difference we need not go into here, their ana-lytic character does not exempt them from justification; for even if it is analytic that action occurs only according to self-given laws, it is not for that reason self-evident.

112. One could object that the argument uses a questionable assumption, namely, that action in general must be understood as action according to law. The assumption is certainly implausible if we think only of laws requiring the same action under all or many recurring circumstances of the same type, if, that is, we think only of resolutions like that to stop smoking or to get up every morning at seven o'clock. Certainly we do not always act according to such rules. Suppose you tire of reading, set aside your book, and head for the swimming pool. This is an action even if you are not following the rule of always going to the swimming pool when the temperature, or your discomfort, rises above a certain degree. You need not have defined a certain class of situations as swimming-pool-appropriate. Only now do you want to go, and you go. But you too are acting according to a law, if 'law' is taken only in a broader sense; for you have a general idea of what you want, and you act accordingly. What you want is to go to the pool, and what you do you do in the way and with the end that this description is true of what you are doing. Your idea of what you want to do is general because various possible courses of actions and events can satisfy it; within certain limits, one will serve as well as another.[219] Because the idea of one's own action is a general idea, and because it orients the action, it may be called a law of action. It differs from certain other laws in sometimes requiring a certain action to be performed not in a number of situations of similar type but in just one individual situation, as in the 'Now into the pool!' case. But this is not an important difference. Whether many cases of application are intended or just a single case, this does not affect the generality that the idea of one's action has relative to the various courses of events that may satisfy it. Whoever intends to do a certain thing does not have in mind an individual thing, the deed, that now has to be moved from the possible to the actual; she has a general description in mind, which she intends her action to instantiate.

113. So broadening the sense of 'law' does not trivialize the claim that actions must be understood as actions according to laws. This claim presents an alternative to understanding action as fulfilling desire. In that view, 'wanting to do something' is modeled on 'wanting a thing.' Whoever wants to do something aims at something; the will is the faculty of desire, and the deed realizes what the desire was aiming at. The idea of action according to law, on the other hand, bases 'wanting a thing' on the model of 'wanting to do something': Whoever aims at something wants to do an action of a certain kind; will is the ability to act according to laws, and the deed instantiates a law. Kant's claim that the will is nothing else than practical reason is a pithy expression of this idea and is incompatible with the idea of the will as the faculty of desire.[220] What can be said against conceiving the will as the faculty of desire is not that we sometimes speak of someone wanting to do something even when the appropriate desire, in the ordinary sense of the word, is absent. We do speak this way, but this does not run counter to the proposal not only to refer to desires whenever ordinary linguistic usage would have us do so but also to explain all willing as desiring. What can be said against this explanation is that it fails to do justice to its object. Wanting to do something is a different sort of thing than desiring something,[221] for desire aims at something that exists, or that at least the person with the desire believes to exist. She reaches for something that seems to be there, and the only question is of whether she will 'get to it.' But if she wants to do something, what she wants does not yet exist and perhaps never will exist, because in doing this thing she may fail. Wanting to do something is rather like having an aim or plan. It is not to reach out for something that is there but to project a performance that has not yet occurred.[222] Another difference: Desire is something that sets in, that comes over a person; one is, for example, seized by a longing for something. In contrast, it makes no sense to say of someone that he was overcome, as it were, by his own will. He himself is the one who wants something. In the case of wanting to do something, we do not have a sense of that intrasubjective dualism we sometimes impute in instances of desiring.[223] This entails a third difference. It is not absurd to speak of a sensible regulation or control of the influence that desires have on acting.[224] How such control is to proceed it may still be difficult to say. But it is absurd to speak of regulating or controlling the influence of the will on acting. Behind the will there lies nothing else that could control it.[225]

114. That action must be understood as action according to laws follows from its intentionality. Whoever does something intentionally knows what sort of thing he is doing.[226] What he does falls under the concept he has of this doing. One is inclined to say that whoever does something intentionally must be able to say what he is doing.[227] But this may not be precisely so, because linguistic expression may be hindered for either trivial or nontrivial reasons without the action thereby losing its intentionality. Whoever does something intentionally not only has an idea, as it were, alongside his doing, of what he is doing; he also acts, and in acting he follows his idea. He does what he does because he wants to do something falling under the concept he has of this action.[228] But intentionality is a necessary condition for acting, at least according to one current sense of 'action.'[229] True, intentional actions make up only a subclass of what we say a person does. They even make up a subclass of what a person does not do involuntarily, that is, things he could have omitted doing.[230] But the remainder, things done not intentionally, but also not involuntarily, such things as causing unintended side effects and things like yawning, sneezing, and brooding,[231] do not merit being called 'actions.' At least here they may be set aside as unimportant. But then it will be true of all actions that they follow laws.

115. I have now reached the end of my series of justifications. That there are actions in the sense including intentionality, and that such actions are not marginal phenomena but appear often enough and in sufficiently significant places to be regarded as essential to our lives, I shall assume without argument. Not that this is beyond doubt. After all, descriptions of the world have been sketched that do not acknowledge intentional action, for example, some forms of determinism. But I shall not pursue any further questions and counterarguments on this point. Looking back, the argument, now in reverse order, proceeding from reasons to conclusions, runs as follows: intentional action (114), action according to laws (112), actions according to self-given laws (110), unique validity of self-given laws (108).

116. Some will reject the argument without examining it, because it makes an obviously absurd claim, namely, that one always acts according to self-given laws; for often we do act according to laws that we have in no way given ourselves, laws prescribed either formally by institutions or informally by fellow human beings. It would be absurd to deny that there are such cases. It is not absurd, however, to press for a description of these cases in different terms, for the reasons given in the preceding argument. And such a description suggests itself. We do not act according to prescriptions; we take them into account. Sometimes the account shows that we do well to act as prescribed. But we are only following a law that we have given ourselves by reason of a more or less thoroughgoing and farsighted consideration of our aims and circumstances. The existence of the prescription and the foreseeable consequences of obeying or disobeying it are nothing more than matters to be reckoned with in deliberation, as are the other prevailing circumstances. The most obvious example of such a consideration is the punishment or reward announced for omitting or performing the prescribed action. How much importance a person places on getting the reward or avoiding the punishment and how great the likelihood that these consequences will ensue are important for determining what kind of action is to be adopted with regard to a given prescription. But the deliberation is not confined to the announced consequences – for example, in cases of people obeying a rule in order to obtain the favor of the one who has decreed it (106). Above all, the consideration is not restricted to determining the best means for selfish ends. Whoever cares for the well-being of certain others will examine what sort of behavior on his part regarding this prescription will best serve them. Finally, in deliberation, a person may completely disregard his own ends, selfish or not, and for purely objective reasons decide to proceed in a certain way with the prescription, for example, the 'noble' obedience mentioned earlier (107). Yet, however he considers the matter, in proceeding under that consideration he is not acting according to the prescription; he is at most adapting himself to it. He is acting according to the rule he set himself in view of the given prescription. Acting on the basis of such a consideration need not be selfish, and it need not even materially differ from what is prescribed; but it is action of one's own will, and only under this condition can it be understood as action. For actions, prescriptions are like natural events. One does not act according to them; one takes them into consideration in determining what to do. The best thing is, of course, to influence them according to one's own plan. It may be asked why prescriptions are laid down at all, if no one ever acts according to them. But prescriptions are laid down not so that we act according to them but that we take them into account. Simply in order to give them greater weight in this account, people often link the prescriptions they make with some announced punishment or reward, and with many prescriptions one can foresee welcome or unwelcome consequences that are not expressly announced. In sum: That we talk of acting according to prescriptions and that such cases exist do not confute the claim that one always acts according to a law of one's own. What we say about these cases – in particular, our talk of acting according to a prescription – can be reconstrued consistently with this claim.

117. Whoever is autonomous in this sense of acting only according to laws of her own is also autonomous in the sense expressed by the principle of autonomy: She is subject only to laws of her own (108). In order to be subject to a law, one must at least be able to act according to it. To use the image of subjection: By taking, when one acts, alien laws only into account, one is above them; so one cannot be subject to them. Of course, it would be foolish to be above them in the sense of disregarding them. But one must be above them in the sense that they do not determine one's action but simply are considered in the determination of action. Alien laws are not valid, because they are mere facts (99).

118. In all of this, autonomy is conceived in a formal sense, contrary to current usage. That is to say, autonomy here is not a property of certain actions, something furthered by certain actions, and the like. Here it is a property of the agent as such; it belongs to the concept of acting. Accordingly, heteronomy is not a property of other actions, but the property of none at all. 'Heteronomy' refers not to some danger but to an illusion. The tendency to restrict the two concepts to certain actions probably derives from that usage of Kant's wherein 'autonomy' refers to something that is itself morally demanded, not, as elsewhere, to a condition on valid moral demands (89). Whether the word 'autonomy' is used in the one way or the other, a confusion between formal and substantive senses, parallel to the confusion in Kant noted earlier (90), should be avoided. In any event, that the concept of autonomy used here is a formal one does not entail that the statements employing it lack content and are irrelevant for elucidating action. The illusion that there is such a thing as heteronomy is itself dangerous.

119. So far the argument for the autonomy principle. Kant now tightens up the principle beyond what has been proved so far, by means of the three words I have set aside up to now: 'and yet universal' (102). One's own legislation, being a necessary condition for valid moral laws, is also to be universal legislation. The first question is, What does 'universal legislation' mean? It certainly does not mean that the laws stemming from it are universal in the sense that different series of actions and events may fulfill them. Universality in this sense already belongs to the concept of a law and does not need explicit mention. The will's own legislation, as explained a few paragraphs earlier (112), is, after all, a universal legislation in this weak sense, too. In speaking of one's own 'and yet' universal legislation, Kant indicates a sense of 'universal' such that self-legislation in itself is not universal legislation but even something opposed to the latter. Just this opposition, however, shows what is meant. If the legislation is called one's 'own,' the lawgiver is being denoted. The phrase indicates that the lawgiver is the one subject to the law. If the legislation is called universal, as opposed to one's own, then this must denote the lawgiver as well. The phrase then indicates that the lawgivers are everyone, that is, all rational beings, as can be gathered from the context.[232] Thus, the strengthened autonomy principle places on valid moral laws the condition of stemming from the self-legislation of the person falling under them, and it further requires that the legislation be such that all rational beings are lawgivers.

120. But this sounds inconsistent. It does not seem that my lawmaking could be the lawmaking of all rational beings. Yet sense can be made of this. If all rational beings decree a certain law, and I, also a rational being, take part in this, then this legislation is both my own and everyone else's. A political idea is operative here (87): the image of a legislating popular assembly. Read this way, the condition that the autonomy principle, strengthened by the universality clause, places on moral laws does avoid the inconsistency. But this becomes too restrictive. There is no such thing as an assembly of all rational beings, and moral laws having to await ratification by this assembly would never come to pass. No other solution is available than to limit universal legislation to the merely possible. The various versions with the words 'as if' and similar expressions show that Kant himself was prepared to mollify the criterion this way.[233] Not that all rational beings actually do legislate a law for my action, but that they could do so becomes the necessary condition for its being a valid moral law. One's own legislation and universal legislation thus differ modally. The argument given for the autonomy principle shows that a valid moral law must actually spring from one's own legislation. It need only be capable of being universally legislated.

121. Kant gives no reasons for tightening the principle of autonomy with the requirement that a moral law must be capable of springing from the joint resolution of all rational beings (102). Yet the requirement can be considered analytic. A moral law can be understood as one a rational, impartially formed judgment would approve. That is, the law would merit assent from all rational beings as such. Kant often argued that moral laws must be rational in this sense.[234] Many modern theories impose essentially the same condition, variously stated, for example, Firth's ideal observer,[235] Rawls's original position,[236] and Habermas and Apel's ideal speech community.[237]

122. The autonomy principle, strengthened by the universality clause, places this condition on valid moral laws: They must spring from the legislation of the person subject to them, but must be capable of being agreed to by all rational beings. This is a necessary condition for moral laws. As Kant says, human beings are subject "only" to legislation of this kind. But it is also a sufficient condition. Kant's formulation can be understood to mean that the fact that a law springs from one's own and universal legislation alone suffices to make it a valid moral law, for the argument for the autonomy principle is stronger than we have heretofore supposed. It not only points out conditions indispensable for valid moral laws but also shows how the validity of moral laws can be understood at all. In any case, it is difficult to see how else but by the human will's own legislation one could explain what is meant by the validity of a moral law. The given argument rules out the possibility that the law exists independently or is posited from the outside. Not only must moral laws be legislated by the person subject to them in a way amenable to universal consensus; the only concept we have of them is that of being the outcome of such legislation.

123. If now the strengthened principle of autonomy does establish a sufficient condition for valid moral laws, then the task we have set ourselves is solved (31), for now we have a procedure for demonstrating the validity of moral laws. It must only be shown that all rational beings would assent to the law in question and that the person addressed actually makes it a law of his actions. And however difficult it may be to show this for any given case, it does not seem impossible in principle.

124. Yet this result does not lend confirmation to moral claims. It declares them null and void – not because now there are no moral laws. From what has been said, it suffices for the validity of a moral law that it stem from the legislation of the person it concerns and that it would be agreed to by all rational beings, and no immediate reason is to be seen why some laws should not satisfy both conditions. The reason is, rather, that there are no valid moral demands, given that it belongs to the concept of a demand that it is sometimes directed at people unwilling to comply. Moral laws cannot be urged against the unwilling, because they obtain validity only from the people concerned enacting them. They have a claim only on those who want to act according to them. It follows that moral laws cannot be used as ordinarily supposed. Because they have force only through the consent of those at whom they are directed, they cannot serve as a weapon against them. Returning to our original example (3): Moral laws do not support any claim made on the child to leave his brother the last piece of candy. If he wants to eat the piece himself, no moral law stands in his way. This is not to say that appealing to a moral law in such cases would be ineffectual, or imprudent, or not appropriate to a moral attitude itself. The claim is that in case of conflict with the child's will, the moral law is invalid, and appeal to it void. To the child's question 'Why should I be moral?' our answer was this: No reasons can be seen (28). To the new question, 'Should I be moral?' (31), we now have the answer: If you want to be, yes; otherwise no.

125. In order to provide moral laws with validity even against the unwilling, one attempted to place the requisite self-legislation in the hands of a somehow 'better' self, a pure self, a completely rational self, or the like (93). In this way, the validity of a moral law could be asserted against someone who explicitly refuses to adopt it, because the law can be approved by all rational beings and *is* approved by himself (i.e., by his genuine self). But clearly this does not help; for, once there are two subjects, the rational self as pure legislator and the ordinary self wanting this or that, we have thrown out whatever gain the idea of autonomy brought regarding the validity of moral laws. Once subjects diverge, there arises a question of on what grounds the pure self's claim should take precedence over the empirical self's claim, and in substance this is just the old question,

'Why should I be moral?' The fact that a person who
wants to do this or that is the same person who makes the
laws – indeed, that making laws consists in willing something, namely, a universal rule for action – alone makes
intelligible the validity of moral laws for the person who
wants to do something. But that identity entails their in-
validity for one who is unwilling to comply.

126. The idea that moral laws cannot be turned as demands against anyone refusing to follow them is reminis-
cent of Kant's doctrine of the holy will. The holy will also
knows no moral demands: "The 'ought' is here out of
place, for the volition of itself is necessarily in unison with
the law" (GMS 414). Actually, this is how the human will
should be understood. Here, too, the 'ought' is out of
place – not because the will by its nature is always set on
conforming to moral law; that would be not action but
indeed a natural process. The reason is, rather, that there is
no law for the will but that which the will itself makes a
law. One might say that, here, will is not "necessarily in
unison" with the law, but the law with the will. Of
course, in applying Kant's concept of the holy will to humans, one would not mean to deny that they sometimes
do wrong. One would deny only that wrongness is determined by some law independent of a person's own will,
and not by a law she gives herself. When deceived, we
often do what we do not want to do, and inability makes
us lag behind our own intentions. The inappropriateness
of the 'ought' here should be understood accordingly.
That 'ought' is inappropriate which is not based on a corresponding will of the person in question. This does not
affect our advising someone what, in her best interest, she
ought to do.

127. True, in any given case it will be difficult to decide
whether a certain action is being demanded of someone in
her best interest or independent of her interests. It is often
difficult to decide whether certain advice is based on what
the person advised really wants or is turned against her
will, perhaps in appeal to some true, supposedly rational,
self (125); for what a person really wants often is difficult
to determine. She herself is not the best authority on this

matter in all cases:[238] She may be deluded. Sometimes we discover only after a long while, and sometimes not at all, what someone else wanted and therefore whether by speaking we have helped him or moralized above his head. But the difficulty of determining this does not count against my proposal. A study like the present one cannot be expected to eliminate the practical problems by providing usable criteria for all individual cases. At best, it can help by providing through its general concepts a better insight into the nature of the difficulties one meets, by dispelling confusions and thereby contributing to fruitful solutions.

128. Moral laws are rules for one's own action that would be agreed to by all rational beings (122). They are valid only for the person who adopts them as rules for her own action. This leads to the question of whether someone actually will adopt them as rules for her action. The answer depends on how precisely the criterion – fictitious consensus of all rational beings – is stated. But we may suppose that some of what a person intends to do, even if certainly not all, will meet the criterion and, conversely, that she will resolve to do some of the things meeting the criterion, even if certainly not all, and not even all that are relevant in the situation. The next question, therefore, is whether someone has grounds for adopting a moral law, that is, for adopting a rule of action to which all rational beings would agree. Now, a person may have all sorts of reasons for adopting a rule of which it is true that it would be agreed to by all rational beings. But I do not see how the fact that it would be agreed to by all rational beings should itself be a reason for adopting it (51). If the consensus of all rational beings were not merely a fiction but a fact, or if the consensus were not merely of rational beings as such but of actual fellow human beings, then one could easily understand that it would have some weight for agents. I do not understand how a fictitious consensus among rational beings should have this weight. Whoever acts also cares about other things than a fictitious universal consensus, and therefore anyone deliberating on the best action to take will also care little about this consensus. Of course, it certainly would be of concern if the fact that an action would find universal approval were something good about it. But it is not self-evident that this would be something good, nor does it seem demonstrable, unless we fall back on some moral law whose grounds for adoption were just the issue. To be sure, a person can set anything as his goal, including that his actions always meet with the fictitious approval of all rational beings, and if a rule obtained this approval, this would be for him a reason for adopting it. But I do not see why this should be a reason and why he should set this as his goal. If he did, his doing so would be a sort of predilection for actions of this form, a predilection one would acknowledge and at most respect, and yet not understand, like a peculiar taste in actions. Certainly some people will argue that each person ought to adopt rules of action to which all rational beings would agree. But then the matter becomes circular, for such a moral general requirement is as unfounded as the particular ones discussed so far. The criterion of a fictitious universal approval may indeed distinguish moral laws from other rules of action. But this property common to rules of action that are moral laws is, except in the special case just noted, irrelevant to anyone deliberating on how he ought to act. There is no need to place moral laws in a special class of rules of action. Moral laws are practically irrelevant.

VI. Prudence

147. For this reason, it is the entire complex of plans and experiences into which a reason for action must fit.
148. The reasons that fit in in a way that makes sense are good reasons for one who wants happiness. Wanting happiness is not a necessary but a general attitude of human beings.
149. Defense of my notion of happiness. Happiness is not a goal of action.
150. Reasons sensibly fitting into the overall plans and experiences of a person are what have traditionally been called reasons of prudence.
151. Aristotle's concept of prudence agrees with that developed here.
152. Differences between the two concepts: Aristotle straightaway defines the prudent man by the aim of the good life.
153. Differences between the two concepts: Aristotle is ambiguous on whether all good reasons are those of prudence.
154. Kant's concept of prudence.
155. Kant's examples: dietetics as the model of prudence.
156. A proposal to replace juridical by dietetic metaphors in moral philosophy.
157. Kant's examples: economy, courtesy, and restraint. The difference between economy as means to an end and as the counsel of prudence.
158. Further examples: Prudence is the ability to advise in times of crisis.
159. Mabbott's concept of prudence.
160. Mabbott's claim that prudence is a morally approved attitude.
161. The claim is mistaken.
162. Objections against the doctrine of prudence. First: Why should one be prudent? Answer: there are no good reasons for prudence; they would be superfluous anyway.
163. Second objection: The theory solves no practical problems. Response: It shows what solutions of some practical problems are like.
164. The theory says nothing about the conditions under which one should try to determine the reasons of prudence in a given situation.
165. Third objection: The criterion of sensibly fitting in is only aesthetic. Response: It is unclear what this means and why it is a criticism.
166. Fourth objection: The theory favors conservative solutions of practical problems. Response: Radical changes are not ruled out.

167. Prudence is irrelevant for someone who regards human beings as radically evil.

168. Fifth objection: The theory takes an individualist view of rational action and undermines the social order. Response: Rational action is viewed individualistically only in the sense that good reasons depend on the will and experiences of the individual; there are such reasons for association and for certain orders of association.

169. The objection renewed: In the absence of moral obligation, social orders are ineffectual. Response: Such a prudential argument does not support morality; ineffectual are those social orders without the power to prevail.

170. Sixth objection: The theory returns to considerations criticized at the beginning. Response: They were criticized as justifications of morality, and they are now free of this function.

171. Foot's new version.

172. Foot claims to have de-mythologized morality. Reasons against this assessment.

173. Two senses of 'moral.'

174. Seventh objection: It is superfluous to state reasons sensibly fitting into a person's will, because everyone knows what he wants. Response: Not everyone knows what he wants; prudence is required for this.

129. So, after asking, 'Why should I be moral?' (3) and 'Should I be moral?' (31), we raise a new question. By the principle of autonomy, one is subject to a moral law only if one gives it to oneself. But there is no reason for giving just moral laws and not others to oneself, for what is distinctive of them, the fictitious approval by all rational beings, is not a good reason for adopting them oneself. The question now is 'What *is* a good reason for adopting a law of action, and what sort of laws will one have good reason to give oneself?' The reasons and laws, of course, vary. But it is not their enumeration that we require. Our question is 'What sort of reasons and laws are they?' We are asking for a specific property of good reasons for adopting a law for action, a property common and peculiar to them, and a specific property of those laws that one has good reason to adopt. The question is not of whether any particular reason is a good one but of what, in general, is a good reason or a law made with good reason.

130. Two terms need explaining here. I shall use 'law' as before in the broad sense, to include any general idea of an action adopted as one's rule (112). 'Good reason' does not refer to one kind of reason as opposed to things that are reasons, but bad ones; it refers to what really is a reason as opposed to what is only held as such. Good reasons contrast not with bad but with merely presumed reasons. This way of speaking suggests itself because 'reason' is often used even when what it refers to is not accepted as a reason. Thus, one speaks of 'reasons that a person has' or of 'reasons for her' and reserves for oneself judgment on whether these 'reasons' really are reasons, that is, whether they are good reasons.[239]

131. The question is a natural one. The questions treated earlier, which demanded a justification or proof of validity, respectively, of moral demands, served to examine what reasons there are for acting according to moral demands (32). It turns out that there are no such reasons (128). There may be good reasons for individual actions or ways of acting that are morally demanded. Perhaps there are even good reasons for all morally demanded actions. But this would be fortuitous because the property of an action being morally demanded does not entail that there are good reasons for doing the action. Now, traditionally the opposing view has prevailed, namely, that an action that is morally demanded will simply for that reason be supported by good reasons, indeed the best reasons.[240] It not only prevails among philosophers, it is also an influential view among many other people. That moral ideas have such importance in the life we share with one another, and especially in education (2), is due to the dominance of this view, and in turn sustains it. So it is a widely accepted way of determining what to do that now turns out to be unwarranted. A person used to determining her action in this way may become perplexed by the foregoing and ask how in the end she is to determine what to do if not under the guidance of moral ideas. That is the question I have just raised.

132. My original example (3) can be treated accordingly. A child who wanted the last piece of candy had been faced with the demand to leave it for his brother. The demand was based on the fact that acting in such a way is morally commanded. The question was of whether that was a good reason for heeding the demand. Our inquiry led to a negative answer. Yet if one sort of reason for deciding to act a certain way in this situation has turned out to be specious, one would like to learn the good reasons. The child could, after the moral demand has been set aside, remain irresolute in his behavior. He may still want to have the last piece, but wanting to do something is, even when moral reasons are not involved, no sufficient reason for deciding to do it. He may now ask his teacher for advice. Whatever advice is given, the question naturally arises about the kind of reasons for this advice. The question is all the more natural as it corresponds to the first question in the moral-demand case, namely, 'Why should one do what is demanded?' Then the answer was that the child should do this because it is morally commanded. Now he is supposed to do what he is advised to because – well, because of something different. The question is, 'What is this different sort of reason?'

133. In Kant's terms, this is the question: 'If not moral laws, what is the direction that practical reason gives to action?' After all, the argument for the autonomy principle does not deny that there is practical reason. On the contrary, the argument is based on Kant's claim that will is nothing but practical reason, that action can therefore be understood only as the exercise of practical reason, as action according to laws (110). What is denied is only that the laws a rational being gives himself are moral laws. The question is, then, '*What* sort of laws do we have reason to give ourselves, and *what* sort of reasons are these?' That is, 'What direction does practical reason give to action?'

134. Plausible as the question may seem, it may still lead us astray. The point is to find out what reasons, in general, are good reasons for adopting certain ways of acting, and it is natural to expect an answer like that provided by a principle of morality, such as Kant's, namely, a rule for selecting maxims. So understood, the question asks for a substitute morality, that is, for a criterion by which to classify proposed reasons for adopting a way of acting either as good reasons or as merely presumed reasons. But autonomy does not permit such a substitute morality either. Whoever is subject only to self-given laws is also, as legislator, subject only to self-given laws. The argument for the autonomy principle applies equally at the new level. Indeed, only a pseudoautonomy would entrust laws for action to the agent's own legislation and yet place this legislation under laws not owing their validity to her. If autonomy holds, no prescription can lay an independent claim to her allegiance, not even some such criterion for good reasons as opposed to merely alleged reasons for acting a certain way. Whether a stated reason is good or not is never determined from the outside.

135. This threatens to make an answer to the question impossible; for what is a good reason and what is not now seems arbitrary, so that talk of good reasons for adopting certain ways to act has lost all meaning. But, in fact, we do not always recognize as a good reason what a person advances as such. We criticize reasons. But this does not make sense if what is a good reason is arbitrary.

136. A dilemma thus arises between autonomy and rationality. It is similar to that in Kant between autonomy and the fact of reason (101), except that it concerns not just moral, but all laws of acting. If autonomy holds, then there seems to be no available criterion for what is and what is not a good reason for adopting a certain course of action; hence, good reasons themselves seem to drop out. If there is such a criterion, however, then autonomy seems to disappear.

137. The rule of action whose grounds for adoption are in question will not be the first rule a person chooses. She already will have adopted countless other laws of action of greater or lesser import that are variously interrelated. They will rest on countless reasons, also of greater or lesser import and variously interrelated. The laws together form a picture of the future activity she intends, and the reasons bear the trace of her experience of life so far. A reason may be a good one depending on how it is related to this complex of projects and experiences that a person brings into her decision. A reason for adopting a certain way of acting as one's rule is a good reason if and only if it fits into the agent's projects and experiences so as to make sense. Thus, a plan may be justified by being shown to fall under a broader previously conceived plan. Or experience may show that some course of action serves an aim already held. Or an intended action may supplement an earlier, more narrowly conceived plan. Or the reason for acting a certain way may provide a whole series of plans with some overarching intention. There may be yet other ways of fitting together various intentions. Moreover, one will have to estimate the opportunities and obstacles that experience tells one to expect in carrying out the plans.[241] So fitting in a sensible way into a person's conception of her life is the mark of a good reason for action.

138. This response to the demand for a criterion for good reasons solves the dilemma of autonomy and rationality. On the one hand, autonomy is retained. What is a good reason for adopting a rule of action is not prescribed. It depends on what the person wants. Of course, it will also depend on how things stand regarding matters that the action concerns. But it is no restriction on autonomy that self-legislation must also take into account the way the world goes (116). On the other hand, that 'being a good reason' depends on the agent's own will does not mean that 'being a good reason' is left to her caprice. What a person wants is not an arbitrary matter; it is already laid out in a multifarious network of intentions. The requirement that good reasons can be embedded in such a network, however, makes them subject to rational deliberation and critique; for this property can be tested by anyone who knows a person's intentions, whether she be that person or some other. In this way, the person can be advised, that is, helped to form a rational judgment on whether or not and how acting a certain way fits in a sensible way into the conception she has of her own life in the world. Nevertheless, such advice will not state good reasons having this status independently of the agent's will and knowledge.

The advice does not constrain autonomy; it supports autonomy by attempting to clarify what a person wants.

139. One will ask what exactly it means to fit in in a sensible way. I shall not give a detailed answer here; that would require a full account of the procedures just mentioned (137) of ordering one's intentions. It would have to be shown what kind of considerations we give weight to in staking out our plans, what kind of reasons we use to criticize our own or another's plans, what sort of insight someone has who learns through being advised, and also what sort of insight someone has who remains steadfast in his project despite others' objections, because he knows that he does best to proceed this way. It would require, in short, a complete theory of how practical reason operates. The technical model of searching for suitable means to given ends does not appear to suffice for such a theory (137). Lacking this theory, one must rest content with a rather loose phrase like 'fitting in so as to make sense.' But a few points may be added to give a clearer picture of what is meant.

140. Fitting new projects into old plans and experiences in a sensible way does not require that the latter remain unchanged. That would be tantamount to making the concept unusable, for a new rule of action will almost never fit smoothly into what the agent has wanted up to then. Meanwhile, which changes merely modify what has been wanted all along and which changes are so profound that they do not fit anymore in a sensible way cannot be stated in general. Persons will judge this matter differently, depending on what they consider important or essential among their prior intentions. That such assessments of intentions will influence the determination of what is a good reason is not surprising. It accords with experience that profound differences of opinion about what to do may sometimes extend to the judgment as to whether a certain consideration may count as a good reason at all. This does not pose a threat to the rationality of such deliberations. If different assessments of relevance come into play, then agreement between these assessments may be sought in the same way as had been agreement between the planned actions themselves, namely, by reference to some broader framework of intentions and experiences. Often, agreement will not be forthcoming. But nothing says that it is ever impossible to reach.

141. We also demand too much of 'sensibly fitting in' if we insist that all of a person's projects must be ordered under a single comprehensive plan or serve a single, uppermost goal. True, a person is sometimes rightly criticized for spreading himself too thin among different plans. But he need not for this reason be set on a single enterprise, as Plato apparently would have him be.[242]

142. On the other hand, that new reasons and plans merely be compatible with old plans and experiences is too weak a requirement. Someone may plan to do many sorts of things that indeed do not conflict with one another but that are so little interrelated that he can no longer recognize himself in the variety of his actions; he loses his identity, as is sometimes said, a phrase equally in need of clarification. This would not be a case of fitting plans together in a way that makes sense.

143. Such fitting can be adequately explained as establishing a comprehensive structure among a person's intentions, old and new – a structure that is coherent. Although 'coherent' is indeed often used in this sense extending beyond consistency, its meaning in these cases is no better defined than is the meaning of 'fitting in in a way that makes sense.'[243]

144. Fitting one's new plans and reasons in a way that makes sense into what one up to now has come to know and want is like incorporating a new bit of knowledge into one's overall experience or fitting new data into a scientific theory. In these cases too, it is a matter of suitably adjusting the relevant items so as to obtain a 'coherent,' that is, not merely noncontradictory, total picture. But in all three cases, fitting things into the larger frame is indispensable. Another similarity is that neither in the first case nor in the other two cases does one entirely start anew, say, after the first wild attempt has misfired, in order to proceed then according to some rational plan. Once we reach maturity, new plans will always be preceded by old aims, new insights by old experiences, and new data by old theories. Neurath's picture,[244] often employed by Quine,[245] applies to willing as well as to knowing: "We are like sailors who must rebuild their ship at sea, without ever being able to disassemble it in a dock and to construct it anew from the best parts."

145. It may be objected that I am not using the picture in accordance with its original meaning. Neurath's idea was that the best parts for a ship are not to be found at sea; one must make do with what is at hand. That is how a scientific language is constructed; one cannot fall back on perfectly precise concepts and conclusively confirmed propositions but must make do with the historically given means of language, which falls far short of such ideals. In the present context, the image is used in a different way: The best parts for building a ship may well lie at hand, but they can be used only to patch up the old ship, not to build a new one altogether, for otherwise one drowns. So it is with what we want: The new plan must fit into one's prior intentions. There is nothing wrong in using an image differently than originally intended. But used this way, the image leads to a question that had been irrelevant to its earlier use: What does 'drowning' mean in this case; that is, what sort of ruin threatens us in the event that we proceed with the ship as if we were sitting in dry dock? This is the question why, as is claimed, a sensible fit is necessary. To be sure, whoever wants to give himself a law of action will already have adopted many others. But he need not therefore fit this law among the others in a way that makes sense. Rather than establish a coherent order, he could throw himself into the new project and stay with it as long as it carries him and nothing better comes to mind. He could, as people say, "go for it." The circumspection of 'sensibly fitting in' may seem superfluous. The statement made earlier (138), that what we want is not an arbitrary matter, leads to asking the same question. Certainly it is not arbitrary in the sense that we cannot now dispose over what our intentions were up to now. But it is not clear why it should not be arbitrary in the sense that at any moment we can leave behind the entire web of what we wanted and planned to do and take whatever direction fancy chooses.

146. The reason is that we want to be happy. The will is not a faculty of desire (113); it does not reach out for this or that thing, but projects a future course of action. People, however, do not confine themselves to deciding on some particular course of action. Sometimes a person attends to the entire life lying ahead of her and ponders whether acting a certain way is still to be recommended from this perspective. Presumably, human beings do this because they are mortal. What a whole future life will look like is a relevant consideration for mortals, and only for them, for that is what one faces and what can be changed by action. But a whole future life that is good – that is what happiness is. The various intentions a person brings into her decision over a given project will together form an idea of her happiness. To be happy is, after all, not something one wants over and above whatever one intends to do in particular. One wants to be happy just in wanting all those particular things one plans to do. The various intentions as a whole circumscribe a good life of which they individually form parts, whether as means to ends, as things that in themselves are gratifying to do, or in some other way. The new intention does not offer a comparable image of future life. It aims at only a single way of acting, however consequential it may be. The new plan cannot replace the prospect of a good life that a person brings along with her past plans, but can only supplement and amend it. For this reason, it is important for her to establish a coherent structure between them and not deal arbitrarily with her own prior will. Losing sight of happiness for the sake of some new project is the harm to be avoided by fitting old and new intentions together in a way that makes sense.

147. This also explains why the criterion requires that good reasons fit into nothing more or less than the entire complex of plans and experiences – nothing less because a reason for choosing a certain way of acting that fits well into a part of what the agent wants may yet come into conflict with longer-ranging intentions. But nothing rec-

ommending a plan that possibly conflicts with the projected happiness can be called a good reason. In moral
philosophy, one distinguishes between prima facie obligations and actual obligations.[246] Accordingly, one might
think of distinguishing here between prima facie and actual
reasons. But to no avail, for the problem was to show just
what is distinctive of good reasons for action (129), and
these will be reasons that really are reasons, not just alleged
reasons (130). So there is no way but to deny the status of
'good reason' to considerations that only partly fit in. On
the other hand, good reasons for action do not need to fit
into any broader field than that of the plans and experiences determining the image of a good future life. To be
sure, nothing prevents a person from setting himself goals
unattainable in his lifetime. Activity in their service is then
what he considers happiness, and reasons for new rules of
action will have to harmonize with these far-reaching intentions. What is excluded is only that a consideration's
status as a good reason should depend on something outside his will, such as the order of things[247] or God's com-
mandments. It is excluded because of his autonomy (134).

148. Reasons for action that as reasons fit in a sensible
way into the image an agent has of her life are good reasons for those and only those agents who want happiness
(146). Whoever does not care about happiness may be indifferent about whether a plan will fit in a sensible way
into whatever else she wants. It is not inconsistent to say
that some person does not aim at happiness, in spite of
Kant, who holds that it is of the human essence to aim at
happiness (GMS 415f.). Hence, it can be proved to no one
that good reasons for action have a claim on him. Still, the
aim of happiness may be "presumed of every human being
with certainty and a priori," as Kant says in the same
context, 'a priori' being taken in the harmless sense of
what can be known without inquiring into the particular
case.[248] So, actually, good reasons for action are addressed
to everyone.

149. It may be denied that happiness can be understood
as a whole future life that is good (146). Happiness, too, is
spoken of in many ways,[249] and certainly this account does

not do justice to all the ways of using the word. But it does capture one current meaning. Aristotle spoke of those who assume that happiness is the same thing as living and doing well.[250] My use of the word follows theirs. Kant explains that "for the idea of happiness an absolute whole, a maximum, of well-being is needed in my present and in every future condition" (GMS 418). In order for happiness to be an absolute whole, it must, on the one hand, include the present and every future state and, on the other, contain a maximum of well-being; that is, it must include all of one's subsequent life and leave nothing to be desired. So the happiness a person seeks consists in his future life being altogether a good life. This definition has the advantage of making the concept a practical one – that is, relevant to deliberation about action – rather than the mere sum of one's pipe dreams. The definition entails, however, that contrary to the Aristotelian tradition,[251] happiness is not a goal of human action, which is already apparent from the absence of any technique for achieving happiness.[252] The reason it cannot be a goal is not that happiness leaves nothing to be desired. There is no reason why a goal should not be perfect. It cannot be a goal because it includes all of an agent's future life. Goals of action, however, must in principle be attainable. Happiness is not attainable not because such perfection is not for human beings but because as long as we live we are not done with living. Happiness eludes our grasp not like something especially fleeting but like the horizon of our field of vision.

150. The concept of reasons fitting into an agent's plans and experiences in a sensible way and so justifying actions that belong to her projected happiness is no new invention on my part. It is the concept of what has traditionally been called 'prudential reasons.' To be sure, the concept does not cover all the things and only those things commonly called such. 'Prudence' is best considered a philosophical term whose meaning is also occasionally rendered in ordinary language by other expressions. 'Prudence' used to be the standard translation of the Greek word 'phronēsis,' now variously rendered as 'practical wisdom' (Ostwald), 'wisdom' (Kenny), and 'intelligence' (Irwin), and of its normal Latin equivalent 'prudentia,' the source of the English word and the similar French word.[253] I shall not, in order to substantiate its correspondence with the idea I have been developing here, present a detailed history of the traditional concept of prudence.[254] It may suffice to review the testimonies of three philosophers – an ancient, a modern, and a contemporary (151–161).

151. Aristotle explains the concept as follows:

> We may find out what prudence is by considering what kind of people we call prudent. Now it seems that what makes a person prudent is the ability to deliberate well about what is good and beneficial for him, not in some part, like what contributes to health or strength, but rather about what contributes to living well in general.[255]

The prudent man is distinguished by his ability to deliberate well. The idea of deliberating ('bouleusasthai') is modeled on an assembly consulting on some matter. There the ability of deliberating well is especially evident if the decision is a difficult one – difficult because the interests calling for attention are varied and not clearly ranked, difficult also because the situation is not easy to survey and chances are hard to calculate. In such a situation, a good deliberator will be one who is able to throw into relief the decisive features of the relevant interests and of the given situation, so that the picture becomes clear and, in the best case, what is to be done becomes self-evident. Aristotle extends this idea to the individual case. A person needs to deliberate well whenever it is unclear to him what he really wants or what prospects the given situation presents or, as often happens, both. Deliberating well then means reaching a clear picture of what he wants and of his situation, so that in the most favorable case a certain procedure turns out to be evidently the one to follow. He then sees reasons for this procedure that he had not earlier seen or had not seen so clearly, reasons that will be good reasons because they result from a clear picture of what he wants and of his situation. The insight acquired in deliberating well, in the favorable case, is such that things fall into place, and deliberation advises actions that are right in the sense of fitting not into the order of things (147) but into what the person wants and what he knows. My criterion for good reasons, that they fit into the agent's plans and experiences in a way that makes sense, thus merely reflects Aristotle's idea of prudence as the ability to deliberate well. And just as the sort of deliberation that for Aristotle is distinctive of the prudent man concerns not some particular goal but an overall good life, so it is the whole complex of a person's plans and experiences into which good reasons for action must fit (147).

152. My account differs in two ways, formal and substantive, from Aristotle's doctrine. The first difference is that whereas Aristotle straightaway defines the prudent man by his knowledge of what contributes to his happiness, I have proposed first to define prudential reasons as those fitting sensibly into the plans and experiences of the agent, and then to claim that this property is what makes them important to one who seeks happiness. My way is more Aristotelian than is Aristotle's, because I start from what is more familiar to us. The various aims we pursue, not the overall happiness we strive after, are closest and most familiar to us among the things we want. It is with reference to them that I define prudence and on their basis that I introduce the idea of happiness. Aristotle's definition assumes that just as we know what it means to be healthy or strong, so we more or less also know what it is to live well. But living well is not a goal like others we pursue (149). We know of it only in knowing of all the various things we intend to do.

153. The second substantive difference is this. I claimed that good reasons for adopting a rule of action will always be prudential reasons (137). Aristotle, on the other hand, does not say here whether deliberating well always consists exclusively in knowing what is good and beneficial for oneself, that is, whether what is good and beneficial for oneself will in all cases be the decisive viewpoint for deliberation. It could be argued that he did think so, because he held, as did the Thomistic tradition following him,[256] that any fully developed virtue requires prudence.[257] But that argument is not decisive. Prudence may indeed belong to all well-advised action and yet not provide the decisive viewpoint in every case. To be sure, what that difference amounts to would have to be explained. Because Aristotle's definition (151) locates prudence in the skillful choice of means not to arbitrary ends but to some particular end, 'living well in general,' it is difficult to see how prudence could belong to well-advised action in any other way than by determining it. In any case, Aristotle's doctrine is ambiguous here. It can be understood as a moral doctrine: Well-advised action is really moral action, described by Aristotle in his discussion of the virtues; prudence plays only the supporting role of preventing mistakes in the performance of what one recognizes as good. On the other hand, prudence can be entrusted with the determination of what a person is well advised to do, and the so-called virtues described by Aristotle can be degraded to the status of mere rules of thumb for prudence.[258] The ambiguity is revealed in that, among other things, Aristotle ascribes to prudence sometimes merely the choice of means but sometimes the determination of the end itself.[259] A corresponding alternative can be seen in the account he gives of happiness, namely, as lying either in theory or in a rich and practical and, in particular, political life. Aristotle declares himself for the former in the tenth book of the *Nicomachean Ethics* but implies the latter in his discussions in the first and sixth books.[260] Obviously, I interpret him in the second way. Prudence is itself the *orthos logos*,[261] insight in every case into what is the right thing to do; and the good life is nothing but prudence realized.

154. Kant calls prudence the "skill in the choice of means to one's own highest welfare" (GMS 416), that is, in the "choice of means to one's own happiness" (ibid.). But this concept of prudence is misguided. Happiness is not a goal of action (149), and so there can be no skillful choice of means to this goal. Actually, Kant himself later describes things in a way tantamount to recalling this definition of prudence. Because happiness is an absolute whole, he says,[262] no one can ever "definitely and self-consistently state" what he understands by 'happiness.'

But that cannot be called a goal of which one has no determinate idea. It is not that just a precise idea of happiness is lacking. We often do not have a precise idea of the goals we pursue. For example, a person can strive for riches without having already decided how much wealth it will take to make him rich. The indeterminateness of the idea of happiness is different. Not only do we not know where, exactly, happiness begins, we also do not know what kind of thing it is that begins there. That is because happiness encompasses an entire future life. But we do not have a determinate comprehensive idea of such a thing; we have only our many and variously interrelated goals. Kant's doctrine of the discursive character of human understanding also applies to practical reason. Whoever wants to say "what it is he really wishes and wills" (GMS 418) must take the detour of running through the many individual things he pursues. Described collectively, no more can be said of them than, to use the common phrase, "All the best!" – which, however, is nothing less than what Eichendorff suggests at the conclusion to his *Taugenichts:* "and all, all was good!"

155. Not Kant's definition of the concept but his examples reveal what prudence is. He cites advice on "diet, economy, courtesy, restraint, etc., which are shown by experience best to promote welfare on the average" (GMS 418). Already, the first example, and the fact of its being the first, is revealing. 'Dietary counsel' here does not mean, as it has come to mean, rules for eating and drinking in order to remedy certain organic deficiencies or illnesses, such as eating spinach in case of iron deficiency or no fat for gallbladder illness. Nor does it cover only rules for warding off disease. Elsewhere Kant does describe dietetics as the art of preventing illness.[263] But in doing so, he has already narrowed the customary concept, which he certainly knew from the tradition of the School. 'Diet,' in this older sense, includes advice for pursuing a healthy way of life. Indeed, one would like to know from a person knowledgeable in these matters not simply how to get rid of a current malady and to avoid it in the future; above all, one would like to be told how best to live as a being having this bodily constitution. This is more than simply being free from evil. It is to be flourishing in one's nature or, as is said, to be in one's element. It is the happiness of the natural being (to join again those who assume that happiness consists in doing well) (149). Dietetics advises us how, in the future, we can live well as natural beings. Prudence, so exemplified by dietetics, can thus, in turn, be understood as the dietetics of the entire human being. Prudence advises a person how, in the future, she can live well, and not just as a natural being.

156. The example of dietetics opens up a larger perspective. The philosophical understanding of an object is embodied in the metaphors used in describing that object; and the metaphors, in turn, set limits on new ways of understanding. For this reason, changing a metaphor that has become prevalent in some domain is of no minor significance. In the theory of practical reason, concerning good reasons for actions (133), juridical metaphors prevail. What is good to do is regarded as something in accord with some law, or at least not counter to it. What is supported by good reasons counts as obligatory. What is not in one's power cannot be imputed to one. Great difficulties impeding execution of what one is required to do are considered mitigating circumstances in case of omission, and so on. The preceding considerations suggest replacing the juridical metaphor of practical reason with the dietetic metaphor. What is good to do is not a case of something lawful, but of something beneficial and wholesome. Practical reason is not a judge, but a physician. A judge declares what is demanded of certain parties, regardless of their desires and will. A physician advises actions that can be expected to lead to a better life. An appeal to rational grounds in questions of what to do would hardly encounter the irrationalist protest against using reason in matters close to the heart if practical reason showed, instead of legalism, the circumspection proper to action on the living and to aid in living well. True, this, again, is no new idea: "It appears, then, that virtue is as it were the health and comeliness and well-being of the soul, as wickedness is disease, deformity, and weakness," as Plato wrote.[264]

157. Kant's further examples – counsels of economy, courtesy, and restraint – should be understood in the same way as that of diet. They show us how to live well, not with respect to health but, say, with respect to money matters or social intercourse. It could be objected that people save "in order not to want in old age"[265] and are courteous and restrained in order to get along with others. But these seem to be goals of their actions, so that prudence does, after all, consist in the skillful choice and application of means. In fact, however, there is still that difference justifying our not calling these things goals, and prudence a kind of skill. The difference is apparent in the contrast between the person who saves to protect himself from need in old age and the one who saves in order to buy a house.[266] The latter has a goal, and it is attainable, and once it is attained, his efforts will come to an end. The former has a picture of how he wants to conduct his entire financial life, and he will never be done with acting in the appropriate ways. He too knows the foreseeable consequences of economy and wastefulness, and what distinguishes the skill of the prospective homeowner from the prudence of the frugal person is not the ability to calculate probable outcomes.[267] The two differ in the range of their considerations. The one knows best how to arrive at a certain point; the other knows best how to conduct his life as a whole.

158. Kant's examples of counsels of prudence are limited to rules of conduct and general points of wisdom traditionally imparted to the young. But if the foregoing is an adequate account of Kant's examples, more significant examples can be added to them. Prudence is no more restricted to counseling in a general way on how to live well than a physician's counsel is restricted to general rules for a healthy life.[268] She can rather advise someone how, given his particular problems, he can have a healthy life. Thus, prudence fulfills its proper function in advising at times of crisis. For example, a person contemplates studying another field, or taking up another vocation. Or someone returns after a long absence to prior relationships to which she can no longer adjust. Or a person succumbs to some

illness, wrecking all her plans. Or death takes away someone with whom a person has been living.[269] In such situations, the person concerned does not see what a good future life could look like. Sometimes, advice does help her:
the advice, say, to follow this path, to keep that in view, to
free herself from this. Such advice is the model of practical
reason.

159. Prudence, J. D. Mabbott argues in his essay of that
title, brings together different wishes or desires into a unified pattern in accordance with their various weights.[270]
To be prudent is to plan in such a way that different wants
do not interfere with one another, but rather support one
another. In the broadest case, this planning extends to
one's life as a whole, thus represented as a good life.[271]
The concept of prudence I have been developing is in accord with this. 'Fitting in in a way that makes sense,' as I
have called it (137, 139), is just Mabbott's 'harmonizing'
and 'achieving a unitary pattern of desires.' Crucial for
both of us is that anyone deciding how to act already has
many other aims with which he must reconcile the new
one, if he wants to avoid working unwittingly against his
own will. Mabbott, too, likens the understanding in question to that guiding scientific theory construction.[272] But
he seems to be inconsistent in maintaining that desires are
what the prudent planner unifies, inconsistent because he
himself had conceded that this harmonizing does not operate directly on desires.[273] Indeed, it would be difficult to
understand how it could, for wishes and desires set in
unplanned, overcoming a person (113). What actually enters prudence's comprehensive plan is again plans and intentions for action that because general themselves, already belong to practical reason (112).

160. Mabbott regards prudence as a morally approved
attribute. This would be odd, he argues, if a prudent person had only her own interest in mind. Prudence, rather,
has moral value because the prudent person's decision for a
certain way of life and a system of goals is a moral decision, and the approval of this decision is moral approval.
Two kinds of moral approval must be distinguished, he
claims, one concerning actions and, derivatively, corre-

sponding motives and dispositions, the other concerning the character attributes one esteems and would like to have oneself. Prudence is morally approved in the second sense.[274]

161. Yet it is a mistake, first, to define prudence as pursuing some selfish interest. It is also a mistake by Mabbott's own definition of prudence, for according to him, prudence requires only the systematic unity of desire, and nothing is said about its content. Second, Mabbott's reason why we allegedly ascribe moral value to prudence[275] is really no reason; for even when the approval of the prudent person's choice of a way of life is moral approval, it is not therefore moral approval of his prudence. Being prudent, he chooses a way of life that will bring whatever else he wants into coherent unity. Not because he is prudent but because he has morally praiseworthy aims does he choose a way of life that finds moral approval. Neither does the distinction between two sorts of moral approval explain why the esteem of prudence should qualify as moral approval. In fact, as argued earlier (134), prudence is not subject to moral approval either in what it determines one to do or in that the determination is one of prudence. It falls under no moral rules to which its determinations would have to conform (134). Autonomy does not allow for any moral rule prescribing whether one ought to be prudent. A self-given law of being or not being prudent, however, would be absurd. It would come too late, already falling in the domain of prudence.

162. The doctrine of prudence runs into a number of objections (162–75). Thus, one could take up the last point and ask why we ought to be prudent. Even if it is true that the good reasons for deciding to act a certain way are reasons of prudence (137, 150), there still is no reason for attending to good reasons in the first place. In answer to the question 'Why should I be moral?', no good reasons for being moral can be found. Matters may stand no better with prudence. The answer is that indeed they do not. There are no good reasons for letting oneself be guided by good reasons. One does not need to be prudent. In fact, however, such reasons in support of the claim made by good reasons would be uninteresting. On the one hand, a person may deliberate about what is best for him to do; then he already knows or is seeking good reasons, for that is just what deliberation is, and for him these reasons are already reasons for heeding them, that is, for acting accordingly. He thus needs no further reasons for considering reasons or for letting himself be guided by them. On the other hand, he may not deliberate about what is best to do; then he is also deaf to possible reasons for being prudent. Reasons for heeding moral demands are different. Whoever does not deliberate what is best to do is, of course, also deaf to moral reasons. But whoever already deliberates what is best to do needs further reasons for letting himself be guided by moral demands. Unlike the question 'Why should I be moral?', the question 'Why should I be prudent?' does not get an answer, and it makes no difference that it does not get one.

163. The doctrine may also seem inadequate because it does not provide definite answers to practical problems or suggest an effective procedure for finding answers. Our child with his piece of candy does not know any better what to do on being told that good reasons are those fitting into his intentions and experiences in a sensible way. An answer to this objection has already been suggested, however (127, 134). There is no such thing as a set of good reasons for action that are given as such for everyone and whose delineation would be, perhaps, a task for practical philosophy. Neither is there such a set for each person individually. What is a good reason depends on what one wants. That is why, when someone asks for advice in a difficult situation, his questions often turn back on himself. Asked for advice, one cannot in such cases immediately tell what are good reasons in the situation at hand. One needs more detailed information about how the person sees the matter, what interests he is pursuing, and what expectations he harbors. One must, in other words, first learn the complex of aims and experiences into which the reasons one seeks have to fit. Only if this is already known through earlier association may one dispense with checking back in this way. Roughly, then, if you want to know what are the good reasons someone has for acting a certain way in a given situation, you must ask that person himself. If you are the person in question, you must ask yourself, and in that case, especially, an interlocutor may be of help. Here, good reasons are like the psychoanalytical meanings of utterances. The person concerned, wanting to become clear on the matter, often will find it advisable to seek another's opinion; but that other person can only help him reach clarity for himself. The philosopher's contribution, in particular, has this value, too, and only this value. That good reasons coincide with reasons of prudence in my sense provides us with no general solution of practical problems that could be used to calculate particular solutions from the data of the case. As always, one must seek the solution oneself, by considering the individual case. But the philosopher's contribution can provide information about what kind of thing one is seeking, and hence about the best way to look. Such information may be of help in the search; for someone who is clear about the object and character of his search, and who does not let himself be misled by irrelevant considerations, may find what he seeks more easily. Thus, the philosopher's contribution is only a special case of advice in practical difficulties.

164. That good reasons for actions are reasons that fit in a sensible way into the rest of a person's aims and experiences does not entail anything about the conditions under which a person ought to determine if they fit. In particular, it does not entail the absurd rule that one recapitulate and renew an entire life's plan prior to making any decisions, no matter how trivial. In fact, we usually decide on the basis of much narrower considerations. There is no harm in doing so, as long as we can take for granted that they also fit into some broader perspective. If that is not so, or if conflicts affecting our chief aims arise, then it is appropriate to ask ourselves what it is we basically want.

165. One may well say that 'fitting in in a way that makes sense' and 'coherent structure' are only aesthetic criteria. But this does not mean much so long as no account of 'aesthetic' has been given. If the word is supposed

to suggest that the question is 'a matter of taste' (128), then
it is misplaced. Whether something does or does not fit in
in a way that makes sense can be judged on the basis of
reasons (129). But if the word means something else, then
it is not clear that the use of aesthetic criteria is so deplora-
ble. Assuming that aesthetic criteria are those that prove
especially informative in judging works of art, it could
well be that similar criteria are relevant to deciding what is
a good reason for adopting a particular rule of action.
Perhaps we recognize in works of art models of the inter-
connections displayed by good reasons for action in the
overall image of our own lives. Perhaps we are drawn to
works of art because they show what a life can look like.
Then they, too, in a broader sense, can advise us on action.

166. One might also complain that the theory, rather
than stating too little, preempts consideration of individual
cases, and for no reason declares certain solutions inad-
missible. It could be charged with favoring a conservative
approach to practical problems. If good reasons for some
course of action must fit in a sensible way into prior aims
and experiences, then radical changes of life are precluded.
Deliberation about what is best to do will be limited to the
search for procedures generating the least possible disorder
in the previously acquired picture of one's own life. Surely
such a strategy will not open the way to a good life. But
the objection rests on a misunderstanding. The requirement that a new consideration must fit in a sensible way
into prior ones does not mean that the latter should be
changed as little as possible. On that principle, a person
might indeed quickly end up with an image of her future
that would no longer display any meaningful unity.
Again, scientific theories develop in a similar way. 'Coherence' often requires adaptation to new data in a different way than that involving the least change possible in the
received theory. Moreover, good reasons for an action fit
in a way that makes sense, not only among prior aims but
also among the experiences the agent brings to the situation. But the latter will sometimes compel her to re-
organize her plans from the ground up. Radical changes in
this sense are therefore not precluded by my concept of
prudence.

167. Reasons of prudence lose significance in the eyes of one who finds human beings radically evil, one, that is, who supposes some fundamental, all-infecting, and inescapable wrongness in human life. Because prudent action is always linked to prior aims and experiences and never starts entirely afresh (144), it can only mean continued disaster to anyone thinking this way. Any hope for salvation must lie outside the circle of one's acquired intentions and experiences. The Christian doctrine of original sin exemplifies this way of thinking. My proposal does not conflict even with ideas of this sort. Someone could grant all that I have said, even my identification of good reasons with reasons of prudence, and yet declare all these reasons void, and worldly prudence folly. The friend of prudence has nothing to reply, for his opponent already considers worthless whatever reasons he might advance (162).

168. The foremost objection may be that the restriction of good reasons for actions to reasons of prudence entails an individualistic view of rational action and so robs the social order of its basis in reason. But the claim that prudence takes an individualistic view of rational action is ambiguous. If it means that reasons of prudence recommend only actions useful to the agent in the long run, then it is false (161). Nothing prevents the prudent agent from setting as her goal others' utility, or even something that cannot be understood as anyone's utility. In particular, that she wants happiness does not prevent her choosing such aims, for it is still an open question where she takes this happiness to lie, and what actions she considers as belonging to the good life. She may even find the good life to lie in dying for something that matters to her. On the other hand, the claim that prudence conceives rational action individualistically may be intended to characterize not the content but the maker of prudence's laws for action. In that case, the contention is true. It says the same as the autonomy principle: Only those laws are valid that a person gives herself. The doctrine of prudence is indeed individualistic in that an action's being recommended by good reasons is said to depend on the will and experience of the individual. Yet individualism in this sense is not objectionable. For one thing, it is not inconsistent with the rationality of actions. The rules an individual sets himself are not for that reason any less amenable to evaluation on rational grounds (138). Second, the consequence that no social order can be grounded on reason can again be variously interpreted. In one sense, it does not follow from the said individualism; in another, it does, not absurdly but acceptably. The individualism does entail that there are no good reasons existing independent of the individual's will for human association or certain forms of human association. Like all reasons, the reasons for human association fall under the condition of fitting into whatever else the agent knows or wants. But some reasons for association and for certain forms of association do satisfy this criterion, and the individualism does not entail that there are no good reasons of this sort. It is not that humans simply ought to live together or live together in a certain way; it is, rather, that much speaks in favor of doing so. Human beings lead a political life not by nature, as Aristotle held, nor in accordance with duty, as Kant thought, but because of their interests, as Hobbes said.

169. It will be replied that mere reasons of prudence do not suffice to sustain a social order benefiting all participants. In the absence of moral obligation, everyone will occasionally break the rules in order to improve his or her standing, and these will rapidly lose their force. But this is a strange argument. First, it pleads on the basis of prudential reasons, or at least alleged reasons, against admitting only prudential reasons as reasons for action (11). Thus, the argument undercuts its own claim, for whatever needs the support of prudential reasons in order to qualify as a good reason will itself be prudential derivatively. Against this it may be said that moral reasons stand without support from prudential reasons, the latter providing only added reinforcement. But it is not clear what it means to reinforce something that stands securely anyway, and the claim that moral considerations stand as good reasons has thus far proved unfounded. Second, the argument puzzles by ascribing to moral considerations such a great influence on human action that their validity is what saves the social order from collapse. That achievement should be expected not from morality but rather, following Hobbes, from some force threatening injury to whoever violates the order (21, 116).[276]

170. Still another objection is that the theory returns after several detours to proposals criticized earlier. Foot has already suggested defining good reasons for actions on the basis of what the agent wants (23). Baier has already appealed to Hobbes's position (20). The criterion of fitting new reasons in a sensible way into old aims and experiences recalls Henrich's idea of an "integrated form of life," of the "broadest and most unified interpretation of human life-possibilities" (12).[277] These are indeed considerations common to the theories I discussed at the outset and the theory I now propose. But they serve different tasks in the two cases. In the earlier theories, they were intended to justify moral demands or to show their importance. In the present context, they help to characterize the good reasons an agent has for giving herself some law of action. My earlier critique showed that Foot's and Baier's considerations were unequal to their task. Their arguments were in effect prudential arguments – acceptable as such, to be sure, but not suited for a justification of morality. Henrich's claim that his idea of an integrated form of life falls outside the domain of prudential reasons is just as unconvincing. Freed from the burden of supplying a proof of morality, a task they cannot perform, these considerations find their appropriate place here, in a theory of prudence.

171. Philippa Foot, however, has revised her theory in her more recent work. In "Moral Beliefs," moral demands were said to be justified on the grounds that everyone has reason – for the sake of his interest or desire – to heed them. But this was not so, and the justification broke down. In her more recent work, she continues to claim that something's being a good reason depends on the agent's interest or desire.[278] True, she admits, it cannot be positively ruled out that there is some other kind of good reason and that moral considerations are reasons of this kind. But thus far it has not been shown that this is the case. That is why Foot no longer claims that everyone has

a reason to act morally.[279] Whether one has or does not
have such a reason instead depends on one's interests. But,
she notes, interests and desires are not limited to selfish
aims (161). Some people want to act rightly and therefore
have reason to do so. The struggle for freedom and justice,
and against inhumanity and repression, is led by an army
of volunteers.[280]

172. The argument I have developed takes another
route, namely, the autonomy principle, but arrives at the
same result: that what is a good reason for action depends
on the agent's interests, and that moral laws do not have
binding force.[281] There remains disagreement only over
what this result means for morality. My theory concludes
that moral demands as such are unjustified and therefore
void (124). Foot, on the other hand, thinks she is not
attacking morality but only ridding it of accompanying
illusions.[282] But it is not clear what the purified morality is
that emerges here.[283] It is not clear what, under these circumstances, it means to say that there still are some goals
that one ought to adopt, as Foot contends.[284] Because such
a rule can no longer be established as binding for everyone,
what the statement amounts to is merely a bit of advice
that Foot extends to everyone. Advice, however, should
not be directed at everyone; it should be given to particular
individuals. But advising someone in view of his special
circumstances and intentions is the work of prudence, not
of morality.

173. True, this contrast may be questioned. The claim
that all good reasons for action are prudential reasons
could be taken to assert the principle of a morality of prudence. But there is no substantial disagreement here. The
term 'moral' is being taken only very broadly, perhaps so
broadly that any statement about what are good reasons
for action will say something about morality. Taking the
word so broadly, to include even what, in Kant, for example, is the very opposite of what he means by it, invites
misunderstanding and should be avoided.

174. Yet stating good reasons for choosing a course of
action may seem a superfluous thing to do. Good reasons,
I claimed, fit in a way that makes sense into what the agent

wants. But she knows already, one will argue, what she wants and hence which new aims do or do not fit. The individual agent, then, who is the appropriate person to be told about good reasons for her actions, will in fact always know them already. So they have no practical import. But it is false that she always knows what her will is. Some people, as the phrase goes, don't know what they want. That may seem paradoxical. If somebody wants something, one is apt to say, she must also know that she wants it – otherwise she simply does not want it but at one time had wanted it or the like. But the paradox vanishes once one recalls the diversity of willing (137). Willing does not consist in aiming now for one thing and later for another. It consists in the extended network of plans, a network continually being repaired, expanded, and simplified. But then it is easy to understand that a person sometimes does not know her own aims and gets caught up in her own, self-fabricated net. That everything a person thinks, feels, and wills must be transparent to her is, after all, an unfounded prejudice. To use another image: A person may no longer know where she is in the landscape of her own will. That is why it is not always superfluous to give a person good reasons for choosing a certain course of action. They may help orient her if she has lost her way. Conversely, then, that person will be prudent who knows what she wants.

VII. Finitude

175. In this chapter, I take up one last objection to the prudence doctrine. Some may find the restriction of good reasons in the choice of actions to prudential reasons unacceptable on the grounds that what it is right and rational to do will then be a contingent matter and any conception of practical reason rendering its determinative acts contingent is necessarily mistaken. The objection deserves thorough scrutiny, for it leads to the metaphysics of prudence. That is to say, answering this objection means describing in some of its aspects the world in which the conception of practical reason as prudence represents us as acting.

176. It should be explained what 'contingent' means here. If the objection is that right action is determined contingently in the sense of not falling under a law that is valid independent of the agent's willing, then the objection does not merit our attention. This contingency is established by the argument for autonomy, and the critic can only counter with the assurance that matters stand differently. Second, the claim that according to the prudence doctrine, what is good reasons for actions is contingent cannot mean that this doctrine leaves up to the agent's caprice what counts as a good reason. Earlier (138), I showed that it does not do this. Which reasons are good reasons is so far from being contingent in this sense that complete knowledge of how one sees one's life would enable one to judge with certainty what are good reasons for one's actions. We usually are not sure of the advice we give others or even ourselves, only because as a rule our knowledge of the relevant circumstances and aims is inadequate, even in our own case. Third, talk of contingency could be explained as follows: If good reasons are restricted to prudential reasons, then whether or not something is a good reason depends only on the circumstances, aims, and experiences of the agent. But all this is contingent; it could have turned out otherwise. Thus, prudent advice is also contingent; in another course of events, other considerations would have counted as good reasons for action. Yet the objection cannot mean this either. Contingency of good reasons in this sense does not attest against the prudence doctrine. On the contrary, any concept of reasons for action not allowing them to vary under changed circumstances is unusable.

177. The following interpretation of 'contingency' opens up better prospects. According to the prudence doctrine, what is rational to do depends on how the agent has experienced the world and on how she wants to live in the future. It depends only on this. According to the autonomy principle, there is no higher-order standard for rational action (134, 147). But then action will be deprived of any context of meaning extending beyond the individual's life. So what could be meant by the contingency of good reasons is that they lack a place in a supraindividual context of meaning for our actions. Contingency in this sense seems intolerable for a conception of practical reason. Understandably enough, it is from such larger contexts of meaning that we borrow many, perhaps most, of the considerations on the basis of which we think we rationally determine our actions.

178. But reasons of prudence are not contingent in this sense. Unclear as the expression 'supraindividual context of meaning' is, in one plausible sense prudential reasons can enter such a context, namely, if it is taken to be some sort of common cause in which many people are acting jointly, for nothing prevents the prudent person from adopting a common cause for herself (161, 168). True, she must adopt it; it is not the case that without her own doing, it is, or ought to be, hers. But there is no reason to suppose that prudence does not allow action to have a context of meaning that extends beyond the individual's purview.

179. Not content with this response, the critic will broaden the sense of 'contingent.' What is good reasons will now already be contingent if it is not a necessary condition for their being good reasons that they fit into a context of meaning extending beyond the individual's own actions. The fact that a person can adopt a common cause as her own does not mean that her reasons for action are not contingent, for she could just as well refuse to join. Good reasons will not be contingent only if, just to be good reasons, they must be placed in such a larger context of meaning. But the rational determination of action, it will be argued, does not permit a contingency of reasons even in this broader sense. Rational determination of action is conceivable only as taking place in a context of meaning extending beyond the individual's actions.[285]

180. The defender of prudence will deny just that. He will argue that there is no contradiction between rationality and contingency, in this sense, in the determination of action. It may be left to the individual's rational decision whether or not common cause will be made, rather than the rationality of the decision being made to depend on the commonality of the cause. Hegel offers arguments against this defense of prudence. He tries to show that a rational determination of action cannot be contingent in this sense, that is, that good reasons for action, to qualify as such, must fit into a supraindividual context of meaning. In his terms, he tries to show that the proper conception of rational action is 'spirit.' His arguments are of special interest in that they are intended not to contradict the autonomy principle. Commitment to this principle is common to his theory and to the idea I have been developing.[286] My dismissal of moral demands on grounds of autonomy (124, 128) reconstructs Hegel's similarly founded critique of the 'ought.'[287] Hegel, however, does not limit the rationality of action, now free of moral demands, to prudence, as I propose. Along the lines of the present objection (179), he charges prudence with determining action in a merely contingent way. And what we now need to be shown are reasons for regarding this contingency as unacceptable. Admittedly, this account of the matter presupposes an overall interpretation of Hegel the adequacy of which may be questioned. I shall not expound and defend that interpretation here, however. The present context allows me to dispense with the elaborations such a defense would require, for I am concerned here with the plausibility of the argument gleaned from the text, not with the faithfulness of the interpretation.

181. The argument for proceeding beyond the contingency of prudential reasons to a spiritual notion of rational action is contained in the section of the *Phenomenology of Spirit* entitled "The Spiritual Animal Kingdom and Deceit, or the 'Matter in Hand' Itself" (PhG 285–301/237–252).[288] We may neglect the two small subsequent sections, on lawgiving and law-testing reason, as inessential to the argument, so that it is the spiritual animal kingdom that makes the transition from the 'reason' chapter to the 'spirit' chapter. Indeed, the spiritual animal kingdom explicitly concludes with the "essence which is the essence of all beings, viz. spiritual essence" (PhG 300/252). This transition marks the central turning point of the book. Up to that point it had presented, true to its original title,[289] a science of the experience of consciousness; that is, it had presented in a supposedly necessary series the ways in which consciousness relates to objects in general, with 'objects' including human beings. Starting from here, it develops a phenomenology of spirit; that is, it sketches a series of shapes of spirit that, because spirit comprises consciousness as well as objects, are shapes of an entire world (PhG 315/265).[290] The section on the spiritual animal kingdom has the task of showing that the overarching reality of spirit supersedes a consciousness relating itself to objects, for it is in the spiritual animal kingdom that the idea of consciousness is fully developed.

182. Two concepts need to be explained first. 'Consciousness' (*Bewusstsein*), which Hegel uses in the *Phenomenology* without explicitly indicating to what the term refers, is best understood on the model of Heidegger's *Dasein*. *Dasein* (literally, 'being there') is Heidegger's term for what others have called 'human being.'[291] In using this term, he makes it clear that the study of human beings in *Being and Time* is a study of what a human being is by virtue of his being there.[292] Similarly, 'consciousness' is Hegel's term for what others have called 'human being.' He uses this term in order to make it clear that the study of human beings in the *Phenomenology* is a study of what a human being is insofar as he is conscious.

183. The second concept, 'reason' (*Vernunft*), has a narrower sense in Hegel than I have given it. Reason, or practical reason, which is my only concern here, is for me the sum total of reasons for adopting certain rules of action, as well as these rules themselves (133). That good reasons for action are simply reasons of prudence means that practical reason is nothing but prudence. In Hegel, on the other hand, 'reason' – again limited to practical reason – refers to only one kind of reason and rule of action. Focusing on the completed stage of reason, which is the spiritual animal kingdom, one can say that, for Hegel, 'reason' means the same as 'prudence.' That is why, for Hegel, a full account of human action cannot be given in terms of reason, in the *Phenomenology*'s sense of the word, but only in terms of spirit. My claim that good reasons coincide with those of prudence can therefore be stated as follows: What I have been calling 'reason' here is in fact nothing more than what Hegel calls 'reason.' Hegel's counterthesis is that reason, in the sense of reasons for actions, is not mere 'reason' in the sense of the *Phenomenology;* in truth, reason is spirit.

184. My claim that the rationality of the spiritual animal kingdom is prudence may seem surprising. True, the word 'prudence' is not to be found in the text, but the relevant allusions are clear. Hegel's spiritual animal is an acting consciousness that knows of no demands opposing it. It determines itself strictly in accord with its own nature:

> The original nature is alone the in-itself, or what could be laid down as a standard for judging the work, and conversely. Both, however, correspond to each other: there is nothing for individuality which has not been made so by it, or there is no reality which is not individuality's own nature and doing, and no action nor in-itself of individuality that is not real. (PhG 289f./242)

This opposition having fallen away, the spiritual animal is called spiritual. Determining its actions strictly in accord with itself, not in accord with some context of meaning extending beyond individuals, the spiritual animal is not itself called spirit, but animal. It moves in its element (PhG 286/238). It need not force through, against the resistance of external objectivity, the certainty that its world is wholly a world of its own action, as the earlier shapes of consciousness had to do. In acting, it only displays itself.

> Therefore, feelings of exaltation, or lamentation, or repentance are altogether out of place. For all that sort of thing stems from a mind which imagines a content and an in-itself which are different from the original

nature of the individual and the actual carrying-out of it in the real world. Whatever it is that he does, and whatever happens to him, that he has done himself, and he is that himself. (PhG 290/242)

Thus, the spiritual animal is a picture of prudence (151). Reasons of prudence, I said, are reasons fitting in a way that makes sense into the plans and experiences of a human being (150). This means that they are reasons corresponding to the original nature of the individual. Because spiritual animals are humans, what is called their 'original nature' cannot be taken to be an initially given and enduring essence. An original nature is the special character acquired by an individual in the course of its history. This nature is called 'original' because it is not posited from the outside but is acquired only in this history of the individual itself. The prudence of the spiritual animal lies in acting only from this nature.

185. The argument leading from the spiritual animal kingdom to spirit falls into two parts. They are linked by the concept of the 'matter in hand,' it being the goal of the first step and the point of departure for the second. In the present context, only the first step need concern us: the introduction of the 'matter in hand.' It is the 'matter in hand' that first confronts the allegedly contingent action of the spiritual animal with something existing and enduring. It is the first object of a reflection of consciousness out of the work into itself, and it ruptures the spiritual animal's accord with its external actions (PhG 294/245–246). For this reason, it is also said to express 'spiritual essentiality' (PhG 295/246). The second step only replaces that with the 'spiritual essence' (PhG 300/252). That is to say, the second step replaces the 'matter in hand,' whose generality lies in the arbitrariness with which different moments of one's action may be brought under this concept, with a matter that is in itself general, namely, a cause common to individuals, a matter that "is such only as the action of each and everyone" (PhG 300/252). It is true that only this step takes us to that supraindividual context of action that can be called 'spirit' (180). But the reasons for leaving the spiritual animal kingdom and taking refuge in a notion removed from individual actions must lie in the first step. The defender of prudence, however, will refuse to leave the spiritual animal kingdom at all, claiming that this is just how human action must be understood. Hegel's reasons for the first step, therefore, are the reasons that must decide between the objection against prudence and the defense of that doctrine.

186. Hegel's critique of the spiritual animal kingdom starts from the produced 'work,' "the reality which consciousness gives itself" (PhG 290/405). The work, he argues, renews the antithesis on which the preceding forms of consciousness were based and from which the present form presumed itself free, namely, the "antithesis of doing and being" (PhG 292/406); for the work, intended to express the individual's activity only, becomes, once displayed, an external thing, "which is obliterated by the counter-action of other forces and interests, and really exhibits the reality of the individuality as vanishing rather than as achieved" (PhG 292/405). The activity and its determination by the nature of the individual turn out to be contingent; that is, they do not matter for the complete work and what becomes of it (PhG 293/407). But conversely, what the work is and what it becomes do not matter for the individual life expressed in it (PhG 293/408). The critique of the spiritual animal's prudence thus consists in denying its existence. "Its empty notion of itself vanishes" (PhG 292/406). Talk of prudence notwithstanding, what action brings about is, after all, external reality, not just the element of a harmonious life plan. Prudence is self-deception. The idea of determining action only according to what a person knows and wants proves to be mistaken because the effects of her action are external to her knowing and willing, not only when plans are frustrated and unintended consequences ensue, but always. "While in my breast the deed was yet mine."[293]

187. But there is no deed that lies only in my breast. Prudence's plan aims at just that reality whose externality is now said to provide the argument against prudence. The harmonious life plan was intended as a picture not of a beautiful soul but of a future activity producing effects in the world. The spiritual animal does not suffer from what happens to its work, as if a hostile reality, interfering from the outside, had thwarted the "peculiar interest" (PhG 292/405) that linked the spiritual animal to its work. The reality that consumes the work is the element of the spiritual animal. If the spiritual animal suffers, then it does so indeed like an animal, from the wounds to its own body; and having been harmed in its life,[294] it will not complain of having exposed itself to the element that made harm possible. There can be no question of a contingency, in the sense described, of the doing as against the work, because the doing includes the work.

188. Hegel himself seems to grant this objection: "Action takes place because action is in and for itself the essence of actuality" (PhG 293/408); reality "is a moment which itself no longer possesses any truth in its own account in this consciousness" (PhG 294/409). But he does not conclude from this that there is no contingency of action and no experience of this contingency by consciousness. He, rather, concludes that "the experience of the contingency of the action is itself only a contingent experience" (PhG 293/408). But, in saying this, he has taken the crucial step. As consciousness, relative to which the experience is regarded as contingent, and its contingent experience separate off from each other, the accord between the spiritual animal and its reality dissolves, and there ensues the 'idealism' "which the 'matter in hand' expresses" (PhG 296/412):

> In this way, then, consciousness is reflected out of its perishable work into itself, and preserves its notion and its certainty as what objectively exists and endures in face of the experience of the contingency of action. (PhG 294/409)

What exists and endures is the 'matter in hand,' which no longer depends on "the contingent result of an individual action, the result of contingent circumstances, means and reality" (PhG 294/409).

189. The soundness of Hegel's argument thus hinges on

the sense in which the experience of the contingency of
doing can itself be called contingent. The argument breaks
down if what is meant is only that some people have this
experience and some do not. Contingency of the experience in this sense is no reason for the insistence of consciousness, against this contingency, on its own concept as
what exists and endures. Generally, an experience that is
contingent in this sense does not merit a place in a science
of the experience of consciousness. Rather, the experience
of the contingency of action with respect to the work may
be considered contingent in the sense that consciousness,
though having this experience in any case, is not affected
by it. It gets over the loss of its work to the world and
remains identical with itself. In this way its reflection into
itself, the return to its concept as what exists and endures,
becomes intelligible.[295] In fact, getting over the loss is just
this reflection.

190. So the question now is why consciousness remains
unaffected by the experience of losing its work. The only
possible answer seems to be that it did not care about the
work anyway; it recovers from the loss because it can
continue nevertheless to act in its element, and this action
is its only concern. But actually this is not so. The spiritual
animal acts in its element, but for this very reason its goal
is not just that, namely, acting in its element, but rather
some work. In consoling itself for the loss of its work with
its enduring 'notion and certainty,' consciousness falls behind the spiritual animal kingdom back into the split that
had been characteristic of "the actualization of rational
self-consciousness through its own activity" (PhG 255–
282/347–393), the split, namely, "into this given actuality
and the end which it realizes by superseding that actuality,
an end which, in fact, it makes an actuality in place of that
which was given" (PhG 261/359). The idealism of the
'matter in hand,' to which consciousness is said to be ris-
ing, is actually the self-conceit with which consciousness
holds fast to the law of its heart (PhG 268–274/367–380).
Moreover, even if the spiritual animal were rightly described as uncaring about the work itself, this would not
explain the contingency of the experience of contingent

action. It would, rather, follow that this experience does not occur in the first place; for if consciousness does not care about the work, then it also has not lost anything, and there has been no loss for it to get over.

191. It has not been shown, therefore, that the experience of the contingency of action is itself contingent. Rather, the conclusion I already suggested holds: Because there is no contingency of action (187), the experience of it is not a contingent experience but simply does not occur (188). It does not occur not because the spiritual animal does not care about the work. It does not occur for the opposite reason (187), namely, that the spiritual animal cares about a real work, and this is a work that is consumed by reality. As a rational being, the spiritual animal does not console itself on the transience of its works with the idealism of the 'matter in hand,' but surrenders itself and its work to this transience.

192. Hegel thus fails to show that action can be rationally determined only through spirit, that is, as brought into a supraindividual context of meaning. Indeed, so far as the argument of the *Phenomenology* goes, there is no good reason for thinking there is any such thing as spirit. It may be true that "the life of spirit is not the life that shrinks from death and keeps itself untouched by devastation, but rather the life that endures it and maintains itself" (PhG 29/32). But such is not our life. We do not endure death, and we do not maintain ourselves in it. Reason, not spirit, is for mortals. True, Aristotle did write:

> We must not follow those who advise us to have human thoughts, since we are only men, and mortal thoughts, as mortals should; on the contrary, we should try to become immortal as far as that is possible and do our utmost to live in accordance with what is highest in us. (NE 1177, b31–44; Ostwald translation)

But no reasons have been given for thinking that what is highest is something immortal. So they are right who advise us to have mortal thoughts, and thus advise 'phronēsis,'[296] prudence, and reason.

193. It would be unwise to deny the notion of 'spirit' entry into practical philosophy solely on the grounds that the *Phenomenology*'s argument introducing it does not succeed; for the philosophical status of the book is dubious, even in terms of Hegel's own system.[297] On the other hand, being told that the system as a whole establishes the claim of spirit will hardly help us decide whether the rational determination of action should be conceived in terms of 'prudence' or of 'spirit.' A study of the system as a whole, if possible at all, certainly is not feasible here. One step in the *Science of Logic,* however, has particular relevance for our question. It is the logical analogue of the argument we have been looking for, the argument for replacing mere reasons of prudence with a spiritual determination of rational action. The step in question is the transition to the infinite in the first book of the *Logic,* for the identification with prudence limits practical reason to the conditions of the finite (146, 192). To conceive practical reason as being in truth spirit, on the other hand, is to free the rational individual from the restriction to considerations fitting into his picture of his finite life (180). It is to place his considerations and actions in a context of meaning extending beyond this finitude. The idea of spirit advances that idealism in practical philosophy that, as Hegel says, consists "in nothing else than not recognizing the finite as a truly existing being."[298] The success or failure of the *Logic*'s argument that the finite has no veritable being thus gives at least an important indication of how the issue between 'prudence' and 'spirit' should be decided.

194. Hegel's argument[299] proceeds as follows. That is finite that not only has a limit but also is what it is only through this limit (*Grenze*) (LI, 116f./129).[300] The finite further relates itself negatively to its limit, through which it is, however (LI, 119/131). The limit, insofar as the finite negatively relates itself to it, is called 'limitation' (*Schranke*) (LI, 119/132). But that as which the finite transcends itself, so as to be able to negatively relate itself to this limit, is called the 'ought' (*das Sollen*) (LI, 120/132). Yet in transcending itself and negatively relating itself to its limit, the finite is superseded, "and what is, is only the infinite" (LI,

124f., 126/136f.). The argument thus consists of two steps, the first from the finite to its self-relation, the second from this self-relation to the infinite. Both need explaining. It must be explained why the finite does not rest within the limits essentially defining it but turns as an 'ought' against its limitation. It must be explained how the infinite can spring from the negative self-relation of the finite.

195. The idea of the argument is stated in Pascal's "L'homme passe infiniment l'homme,"[301] with the difference that Hegel extends it from human beings to the finite in general. Human beings, or finite things, transcend their own limits; they transcend themselves because they are defined by these limits. This is not the trivial idea celebrated as the 'dialectic of the limit,' namely, that drawing a limit or referring to it does not itself belong to what the limit bounds, and in this sense transcends it. It is the bold notion, 'dialectic of limitation' if you like, that something having a limit is itself opposed to that limit and transcends it as well as itself.

196. Hegel arrives at the negative relation of the finite to its limit by considering the following:

> But further, since the otherness is determined as *limit,* as itself negation of the negation, the otherness immanent in the something is posited as the connection of the two sides, and the unity with itself of the something which possesses both determination and constitution, is its relation turned towards its own self, the relation of its *implicit* determination to the limit immanent in the something, a relation in which this immanent limit is negated. (LI, 119/131f.)

The two sides in question are determination and constitution. At the beginning of the paragraph, one reads that "determination and constitution showed themselves as sides for external reflection" (LI, 119/131). Determination is what something is in itself and what it maintains and makes hold good in what it is for another (LI, 119/123). Constitution is what something is, not in itself but only for another (LI, 111/123f.). Talk of an otherness immanent in something refers to the idea that the determination of something reveals itself in what it is for another. What it is for another is an otherness with respect to what it is in itself. But it is an immanent otherness because the determination of something is immanent in it. The sentence I quoted can therefore be rewritten: Because the otherness is determined as limit, as itself negation of the negation, the determination that maintains itself in the being-for-other and has constitution, entirely being-for-other, as something else beside it, is replaced by the determination negatively related to the being-for-other, which determination therefore does not allow constitution to stand with equal validity beside itself but precludes it from defining what something is, so that the unity of the thing consists simply in this splitting into determination and constitution, of which it is the one insofar as it is not the other. The question now is why this negative self-relation enters. The antecedent clause of the quoted sentence does provide an answer: It enters because the otherness is determined as limit, as itself negation of the negation. But at first, this answer seems unintelligible.

197. Before explaining the answer, an example may help to clarify the question. It is the example of moral demands. Granted the 'ought' does not refer in the argument sketched to moral demands; nevertheless, they illustrate the logical state of affairs in a helpful way. In terms of this example, the question is this: How is it that a person turns with moral demands against herself, disavows her manifest doings (i.e., her constitution), and sets what she genuinely is, her determination, beyond this? One would think that no one would be so mad. True, if the demands were established externally and the determination imposed so as to lie beyond how she is constituted, then there would be nothing odd about the matter. But that a person so splits herself in two needs explaining; similarly, the duality of the finite with itself.

198. This, by the way, supports the claim I made earlier without argument: that Hegel holds fast to the autonomy principle (180). If moral laws did not have to be self-given, then moral demands would not be suited for illustrating the 'ought' treated in the *Logic;* for what matters for the 'ought' in the *Logic* is that the one at whom it is directed is the one who posits it. But Hegel's way of expressing himself in the *Logic* would be extraordinarily misleading if moral demands could not even count as an example of the 'ought' treated there.

199. That "the otherness is determined as limit, as itself negation of the negation" (LI, 119/131) should be understood in the following way as the reason for the duality of the finite with itself: That the finite not only has a limit but also is what it is through this limit has the effect that the finite exhausts itself in its otherness. Otherness is not merely immanent in it in the sense that what it is in itself appears in its otherness. Henceforth it is entirely taken up in its externality. The statement that otherness is determined as "itself negation of the negation" means just this. "Negation of the negation" stands for the being-in-itself of the something (cf. LI, 102, 113/115, 126), and so the sentence says this: What something is in itself is nothing but its exterior. With the concept of the limit, victory is given to constitution, and determination is thrust out of the finite. The limit indicates that the finite actually determines itself not through its determination but only through its constitution. That is why what it is in itself now lies beyond it. It is not what it is in itself. Determination and constitution, resting indifferently beside one another, thus diverge into a being-in-itself of the finite, which the finite is not, and into its nonbeing, which it is, so that it only constitutes their opposition. The former is the 'ought'; the latter, the limitation.

200. This also makes clear what is intended in the second step of the argument (194). Through the exile of its determination, the finite is split in two. Whatever is finite *is* only insofar as it is not what it is. Hence, it is not in truth.[302] What is in truth is its opposition in itself and so its dissolution. This last, however, is not something finite. Hence, what is in truth is infinity. The second step therefore does not aim at positing, besides finite things, some other thing having the property of infinity. There is no infinite something. Hegel's talk of a presently won "identity with itself" that is "affirmative being" (LI, 125/137) lets this be easily misunderstood.[303] He seems to grant the infinite a pacified existence beyond the duality of the finite, whereas it actually simply is this duality. Also misleading is his statement that the "finite in its ceasing-to-be, in this negation of itself, has attained its being-in-itself, is united with itself" (LI, 124f./136). This seems to mean that the ceasing-to-be of the finite corresponds to the presupposed concept of it, and thus, as it were, serves it right, which would be an external, hence irrelevant, reflection. The infinite does not rise above the finite and leave it behind, but consists in the splitting of the latter. Pascal's statement that man infinitely transcends man (195) agrees with this; only the transcending is infinite.

201. But the first step of the argument is erroneous. If because of the limit the finite is taken up in its otherness, its determination, which is being-in-itself, need not therefore be posited beyond it, with the consequence that the finite, as this determination that it is not, negatively relates itself to itself in its constitution. The argument passes over the more natural solution that the limit not only, as Hegel says, 'supersedes' (*aufhebt*) a being-in-itself, so that the latter would still have to be dragged along, but altogether annihilates it. The finitude of existence belies any being-in-itself. What is finite exhausts itself in its exterior. Its determination does not fall beyond itself and become an 'ought,' but vanishes. The finite does not have any determination. It freely passes into its manifold constitution.

202. Why Hegel accedes to the paradoxical solution of the finite's duality with itself seems to admit only a historical explanation. After all, it is *une querelle des anciens et des modernes* that underlies the opposition of determination and constitution. Impressed by the undertaking of the moderns to characterize things exhaustively by what they are externally, Hegel does not yet relinquish the ancients' idea that things have a prior determination. He thus leaves what a thing is up to constitution, but holds fast to a determination only falling beyond the thing. The same may well apply to my example (197). Whoever turns moral demands against himself that are independent of anything he knows, wants, or does may indeed understand himself in terms of these doings and yet stick to the idea of there being a determination he has to fulfill. But because in this example and in the logical case the result turns out to be contradictory, it is preferable to accede without reservation to the moderns' claims and, in the example at hand, to entrust oneself entirely to one's manifold life and its reason.

203. Hegel speaks of a sadness that accompanies the thought of the finitude of things (LI, 117/129). With Hölderlin, one could reply:

> In jüngern Tagen war ich des Morgens froh,
> Des Abends weint ich; jetzt, da ich älter bin,
> Beginn ich zweifelnd meinen Tag, doch
> Heilig und heiter ist mir sein Ende.[304]

Notes

1 Plato, *Phaedo* (64a).
2 Hegel, in a manuscript from 1801–2, quoted in Baum and Meist, "Durch Philosophie leben lernen" (pp. 45f.). The text will appear in Volume 5 of the *Gesammelte Werke.*
3 Gadamer, "Über die Möglichkeit einer philosophischen Ethik"; Ritter, "Moralität und Sittlichkeit"; Ritter, "'Politik' und 'Ethik' in der praktischen Philosophie des Aristoteles."
4 Sandel, *Liberalism and the Limits of Justice* (see, e.g., pp. 62–4, 79–81, 141–54, 173f.); Walzer, *Spheres of Justice* (chaps. 1 and 13). Cf. also R. Rorty, "The World Well Lost," and Kekes, "Moral Conventionalism."
5 Ritter, "Moralität und Sittlichkeit" (p. 306).
6 In his explanation of the concept of the ethical order (*Sittlichkeit*), Höffe begins with the phenomenon of 'social protest' ("Sittlichkeit." In *Handbuch philosophischer Grundbegriffe*).
7 This is attested by the problems von Wright encounters in his treatment of this question (*Norm and Action,* chap. VII).
8 Hare, *The Language of Morals* (chap. 11).
9 Kupperman, *The Foundations of Morality* (chap. 1, especially pp. 6f.).
10 *Phänomenologie des Geistes* (p. 302) (Miller trans., §421).
11 In substance, the question is not a new one (§20–26); see also Forschner, "Klugheit versus Moralität," 1.3. But the formulation 'Why be moral?', with its light tone of rebelliousness, is probably rather recent, even if it too does not stem only from contemporary discussion, and research into its origin would be instructive. The earliest record of which I am aware is from 1845: Whewell, *Elements of Morality* (§75). Of interest may be J. F. Stephen's *Liberty, Equality, Fraternity* (p. 275), from 1873, where it is called the most

difficult and important of the great questions of ethics (p. 276). In Sidgwick, *Methods of Ethics* (introduction §3), and Bradley, *Ethical Studies* (essay II), the question already seems current and natural.

12 Nielsen, "Is 'Why Should I Be Moral?' an Absurdity?" (p. 27), mentions this meaning of the question; it is discussed in Mitchell, "Warum soll ich sittlich sein?" (p. 122), and Sidgwick, *Methods of Ethics* (introduction, §3), also seems to mention it. Singer, *Generalization in Ethics* (X.3), entitles his discussion of 'Why should I be moral?' 'The question of motivation'; similarly, Mackie, *Ethics* (8.7).

13 See, for example, Ryle, *The Concept of Mind* (chap. 4); Anscombe, *Intention* (§12–14); Peters, *The Concept of Motivation;* Kenny, *Action, Emotion and Will* (chap. 4).

14 Cf. Kenny, *Action, Emotion and Will* (pp. 85–7).

15 Cf. Melden, *Free Action* (p. 83); Kant, *Kritik der praktischen Vernunft* (*Gesammelte Schriften,* V, pp. 72, 79, as well as Refl. 1021 in XV, pp. 457f.).

16 See Singer, *Generalization in Ethics* (X.3), and Henrich, "Die Deduktion des Sittengesetzes" (X).

17 Cf. Hospers, "Why Be Moral?" (p. 746), and Nielsen, "Why Should I Be Moral?" (p. 758).

18 See Nielsen, "Why Should I Be Moral?" (p. 751), and Mitchell, "Warum soll ich sittlich sein?" (pp. 123f.).

19 The 'institution of promising' referred to in Searle, *Speech Acts* (pp. 188f.), and in the ensuing discussion gives rise to similar misgivings. They are not foreign to Searle himself; see *Speech Acts* (p. 51), where he speaks of "institutions" rather than of institutions. See also Mackie's discussion, *Ethics* (3.4).

20 This distinction is clearly made in G. J. Warnock. His study treats the 'object of morality,' what morality is good for (see especially p. 16), not the reasons for adopting moral valuations and acting according to them. Mackie, who follows Warnock in this matter, still tends to blur the distinction (*Ethics,* 5.1), and similarly for Tugendhat, "Retraktionen" (pp. 162f.).

21 This point will become important when I come to Baier's proposed answer (20–22).

22 Henrich, "Die Deduktion des Sittengesetzes" (X). On the concept of the importance of morality, cf. Warnock, *The Object of Morality* (pp. 157–9).

23 Cf. Singer, *Generalization in Ethics* (X.3), and Höffe, "Kants kategorischer Imperativ" (pp. 97f.).

24 Carnap, "Empiricism, Semantics and Ontology."

25 Cf. Beck, "Das Faktum der Vernunft" (pp. 271f. and 276f.).

26 Thus, the question is that of a 'justification of morality,' a phrase not entirely clear but long current in the philosophical tradition.

27 Thus, J. F. Stephen claims that "the question itself cannot be put except in a form which assumes that the utilitarian answer is the only one which can possibly be given" (*Liberty*, p. 276). His argument is that "the words 'why should I' mean 'what shall I get by.'" But they do not really mean this. Talk of an 'ought' that is justified otherwise than in the utilitarian way cannot simply be ruled out as linguistically incorrect.

28 So, too, McDowell in reference to the word 'should': "The Role of Eudaimonia" (8–9).

29 See also Nielsen, "'Why Should I Be Moral?' Revisited" (pp. 82f.).

30 Baier, *The Moral Point of View* (p. 314). Cf. Mackie, *Ethics* (5); Fischer, "Why Should I Be Just?"; Kupperman, *The Foundations of Morality* (2).

31 N. Cooper, *The Diversity of Moral Thinking* (15).

32 The classical example of this is found in the story of Gyges, which Plato has Glaucon tell in Book 2 of the *Republic*.

33 A similar objection applies to D. Gauthier's attempt to prove the superiority of what he calls 'agreement-constrained utility-maximization' over 'straightforward utility-maximization' ("Reason and Maximization"). He bases his argument on a questionable principle, namely, that choosing a particular conception of rationality is rational only if it is also rational under just this conception (p. 429). But even granting this, there still is no reason why it would not be better actually to be a straightforward maximizer while giving the appearance of agreement-constrained maximization. See also Sobel, "Interaction Problems of Utility Maximizers."

34 Similarly, Monro's critique in his review of Baier's book; also Hospers, "Why Be Moral?" (p. 743); Nielsen, "Why Should I Be Moral?" (pp. 754, 757); Gauthier, *Practical Reasoning* (p. 107); Frankena, *Ethics* (p. 97); Nielsen, "'Why Should I Be Moral?' Revisited" (p. 84).

35 Cf. my critique of Hobbes's argument in *Hobbes' Staatskonstruktion*.

36 Baier, "Moral Reasons and Reasons to Be Moral" (pp. 245–6).

37 A similar direction is taken by Wertheim, "Morality and Advantage"; Reibenschuh, "Warum moralisch sein?"; Meerbote, "Kant on Freedom" (p. 71).

38 Similarly, Foot herself, in a new work, *Virtues and Vices* (pp. 8–10).

39 Hospers, "Why Be Moral?" (pp. 730–7), argues this point in detail.

40 So, too, D. Z. Phillips in his critique of Foot, "Does It Pay to Be Good?"; Sidgwick, *Methods of Ethics* (book 2, chap. 5), makes substantially the same point.

41 "Moral Beliefs" (p. 129).

42 "Morality as a System of Hypothetical Imperatives" (p. 160, along with note 6). Cf. also the introduction to *Virtues and Vices* (p. XIII).

43 Bradley, *Ethical Studies* (essay II); Sidgwick, *Methods of Ethics* (introduction, §3); Paton, *The Good Will* (p. 380). It is noteworthy that Paton, while calling the question absurd, still takes it to be the question of the ultimate justification of morality (p. 379) – which sounds like an entirely meaningful question.

44 So Sidgwick and Paton in the passages just mentioned. Whewell, *Elements of Morality* (§75), also allows only a tautological answer, but does not declare the question absurd.

45 Bradley, *Ethical Studies* (essay II, pp. 58, 61); on this, see the critique in Snare, " 'Should I Be Moral?' " (p. 506). More recently, D. Z. Phillips, "In Search of the Moral 'Must' " (p. 152), and McDowell, "Are Moral Requirements Hypothetical Imperatives?," have expressed views similar to Bradley's. McDowell writes, "The question 'Why should I conform to the dictates of morality?' is most naturally understood as asking for an extra-moral motivation which will be gratified by virtuous behaviour. So understood, the question has no answer" (p. 22). But that this is the most natural understanding of the question is not clear, especially in view of McDowell's own remark that there is a sense of 'should' that is neutral with respect to the division of reasons for action into moral, aesthetic, and so on. See note 28.

46 Brock, "The Justification of Morality." Hospers, "Why Be Moral?" (pp. 745f.), draws a similar consideration.

47 For example, Art. 31 of the West German Basic Law: "Federal law overrides state law."

48 Brock indeed insists on this ("The Justification of Morality," p. 73), and as an example of the sort of reasons by means of which one can try to justify moral demands, he

chooses reasons of self-interest, which can easily conflict with moral demands.

49   This critique is like that in theoretical philosophy that Schaper ("Arguing Transcendentally") has directed against Körner ("The Impossibility of Transcendental Deductions"). Snare ("'Should I Be Moral?'") counters the argument for the meaninglessness of the question 'Why be moral?' by distinguishing between moral reasons as overriding and as fundamental. That is to say, even if moral demands always override other considerations in case of conflict, this does not mean that their claim cannot in turn be justified with other reasons.

50   See Toulmin, *The Place of Reason in Ethics* (11.9); Singer, *Generalization in Ethics* (X.3); Hospers, "Why Be Moral?" (pp. 743–5). Cf. also Hegel, *Phänomenologie des Geistes* (pp. 311f.) (Miller trans., §437).

51   Such tautological formulations appear in all of the passages cited in the preceding note. Cf. also Whewell, *Elements of Morality* (§75), and Nielsen, "Why Should I Be Moral?" (p. 752).

52   See Bradley, *Ethical Studies* (p. 62). Cf. Hospers, "Why Be Moral?" (p. 745); also Hegel, *Phänomenologie des Geistes* (p. 311) (Miller trans., §437).

53   This direction seems to be taken by B. Williams, "Internal and External Reasons," and Tugendhat, "Drei Vorlesungen" (pp. 76f.).

54   That principles characterized as moral still need proofs of their validity has been stressed in P. Taylor, "On Taking the Moral Point of View" (p. 36).

55   Raz, "Voluntary Obligations and Normative Powers" (p. 95). Cf. also Kuhlmann, "Zur logischen Struktur transzendentalpragmatischer Normenbegründungen" (pp. 17f.).

56   Wildt, *Autonomie und Anerkennung* (p. 266), probably goes too far in immediately identifying the two. His attempt to prove the "structural necessity of believing that it is right" to act according to moral norms (ibid.) is cogently criticized by Wolf, *Das Problem des moralischen Sollens* (VI.2b).

57   See Aristotle's *Politics* (1253a 9f and a 2f). On this, cf. Höffe, "Grundaussagen über den Menschen bei Aristoteles."

58   Hare, *The Language of Morals* (11).

59   Frankena, "The Concept of Morality" (pp. 688f.).

60   In a similar vein, Darwall (*Impartial Reason*) more recently has claimed that the validity of moral demands can be demonstrated from the nature of practical reason. But Gewirth

at least gives an argument, even if an inadequate one, for his claim that in making any practical judgment based on reasons one is also committed to judging what under certain conditions every agent should do. Darwall simply takes this for granted (*Impartial Reason,* 13.7–14.5), which makes his account worthless.

61 The argument is developed in the second chapter of the book, under the title "The Normative Structure of Action."

62 *Reason and Morality* (2.7–2.16, in particular pp. 71–3 and 79f.). The same critique is found in Adams, "Gewirth on Reason and Morality" (pp. 583f.), and in MacIntyre, *After Virtue* (pp. 64f.). See also White, "On the Normative Structure of Action."

63 *Reason and Morality* (2.1).

64 On this topic generally, see the anthology edited by Oelmüller, *Transzendentalphilosophische Normenbegründungen.*

65 First in "Justifying Moral Principles" (1958), then more precisely in "Ultimate Moral Principles: Their Justification" (1967).

66 Hare, *The Language of Morals* (11).

67 Lorenzen, *Normative Logic and Ethics* (p. 15); Kambartel, "Wie ist praktische Philosophie konstruktiv möglich?" (pp. 11–13); Lorenzen, "Letter to Kambartel."

68 Apel, "Das Apriori der Kommunikationsgemeinschaft und die Grundlagen der Ethik." Apel has expanded on this idea in many subsequent writings; see, for example, "Lässt sich ethische Vernunft von strategischer Zweckrationalität unterscheiden?" and "The Question of the Rationality of Social Interaction." Cf. also Kuhlmann, "Reflexive Letztbegründung." From the point of view of transcendental philosophy, Krings ("Empirie und Apriori") and Simons ("Transzendentalphilosophie und Sprachpragmatik") have critically dealt with Apel.

69 Habermas, "Zwei Bemerkungen zum praktischen Diskurs" (p. 339). Habermas endorsed the weaker thesis of Apel and the Erlangen School in "Vorbereitende Bemerkungen zu einer Theorie der kommunikativen Kompetenz" (pp. 136–41) and in *Wahrheitstheorien* (pp. 252–9). Habermas's most recent version, "Diskursethik," seems to retreat from the strong position he held in "Zwei Bemerkungen." He now says that presuppositions of argument cannot be straightaway considered valid for communicative contexts (p. 96). The program of an ethics of discourse now seems merely to require that norms be justified in discourses.

How, i.e., on the basis of what, they should be justified remains unclear, though.

70 I pass over Strawson's presupposition relation (*Introduction to Logical Theory*, p. 175), for these transcendental claims cannot mean that every being of whom we can meaningfully assert or even merely deny participation in rational communication must acknowledge rational principles. After all, stones too can sensibly be said not to engage in rational communication.

71 Thus does Kant distinguish analytic from synthetic judgments [*Kritik der reinen Vernunft*, A7/B11 (*Gesammelte Schriften*, III, p. 33; IV, p. 20)].

72 Watt, "Transcendental Arguments and Moral Principles," criticizes transcendental arguments in moral philosophy from another angle. He does not question the presupposition relation, but considers that the skeptic could give up the principles or activities supposedly resting on these presuppositions and in this way escape transcendental arguments.

73 Here he follows Winch, *The Idea of a Social Science*, who attempted to derive from Wittgenstein a new way of understanding the social sciences.

74 That the concepts are amenable to an understanding between the members of a society I take to be the property Norman refers to by the term 'public.'

75 See *Reasons for Actions* (p. 67).

76 Cf. *Reasons for Actions* (pp. 80f.).

77 Cf. *Reasons for Actions* (p. 67).

78 Cf. the discussion of the corresponding theoretical problem, namely, the possibility of alternative conceptual schemes, for example, Rorty, "The World Well Lost," and Davidson, "On the Very Idea of a Conceptual Scheme."

79 The numerals in parentheses refer here and through Section 46 to chapter and paragraph of *The Possibility of Altruism*.

80 To be sure, the final chapter of the book seems to retreat from this strong claim.

81 Similarly, Tugendhat, "Retraktationen" (p. 162).

82 Cf. Gewirth's similar aim in his argument (section 35 above), an aim that he wanted to achieve directly, whereas Nagel relies on the idea of oneself as one person among others.

83 Here Nagel comes close to Singer, *Generalization in Ethics*, and also to the Erlangen School; see, for example, Lorenzen, "Szientismus versus Dialektik" (pp. 71f.), and Schwemmer, *Philosophie der Praxis* (10.2 and 10.3).

84 So Nagel's own statement (XIII, 1). It is often overlooked how easy it is to adopt only objective reasons (see, for example, Darwall, 11, 2–5); one need only dispense with personal pronouns in stating reasons for actions.

85 Nagel no longer regards the argument discussed here as sound (*The View from Nowhere,* VIII, 5).

86 See Höffe, "Zur vertragstheoretischen Begründung politischer Gerechtigkeit" (p. 198). The classical statement of this question occurs in the beginning of Rousseau's *Contrat social.*

87 In discussing Rawls, I refer mainly to *A Theory of Justice* (§18–19, where the principles of moral demands are stated, and §51–52, where they are justified).

88 *A Theory of Justice* (pp. 122–4, 334).

89 Ibid. (§25).

90 Ibid. (pp. 119, 121).

91 Ibid. (p. 121).

92 Rawls is himself clear on this point (ibid., p. 334).

93 Ibid. (pp. 334–7).

94 Ibid. (pp. 337–9 and §52).

95 Cf. Hare, "Rawls' Theory of Justice" (pp. 106f.).

96 Similarly, Patzig in his review of Rawls's book (p. 65), and Harman, *The Nature of Morality* (p. 91). The opposite intuition comes to the fore in Nagel: "If we can make judgments about how we should live even after stepping outside of ourselves, they will provide the material for moral theory" (*The View from Nowhere,* VIII, 1). Even assuming we understand what it means "to step outside of ourselves," what makes judgments arrived at in this way meaningful remains a mystery.

97 See, however, *A Theory of Justice* (p. 21): "We shall want to say that certain principles of justice are justified because they would be agreed to in an initial situation of equality." Cf. further pp. 13, 118, 348.

98 "Kritische Einführung in Rawls' Theorie der Gerechtigkeit" (sect. V).

99 *A Theory of Justice* (p. 21). The passage reappears partly reworded in the book's final paragraph.

00 Dworkin, "The Original Position," which also starts out from the question of why the choice of a principle proves its validity, states some features of the theory that could have provided a foundation for Rawls's use of the original choice and in particular for the questionable conclusion. This theory would have to be worked out in order for the question Rawls himself calls natural to be answerable.

101 *A Theory of Reasons for Action* (1971).
102 Ibid. (p. 80); cf. Rawls, *A Theory of Justice* (p. 348). Recently, Darwall, *Impartial Reason* (15, 6–7), again employed an original blindman's buff to fix a content for rationality.
103 *A Theory of Reasons for Action* (chaps. 8–11).
104 Ibid. (pp. 214f., 15f.).
105 Thus, P. Taylor, "On Taking the Moral Point of View" (p. 58), even holds that accepting this concept of the validity of moral norms is a matter of an attitude incapable of justification.
106 Chapter 14 dismisses the question 'Why should I be moral?' as meaningless.
107 *The Grounds of Moral Judgment* (1967).
108 Ibid. (pp. 88f.).
109 Ibid. (pp. 12, 15–19, 25f.).
110 This is the argument, rearranged, that Grice presents with undue complication (ibid., pp. 94–8).
111 Ibid. (pp. 90f.).
112 The point here derives from an objection that Bayles raised against Singer ("Singer's Moral Principles and Rules").
113 *The Grounds of Moral Judgment* (pp. 2, 57–63, 74–9, 84–6).
114 Similarly, G. J. Warnock in his review of the book.
115 Ilting, "Anerkennung" (p. 361).
116 The distinction between volition and predication of a state of affairs is similar to Hare's distinction between phrastic and neustic components of a sentence (*The Language of Morals,* 2.1), to which Ilting indeed refers in "Anerkennung" (p. 358, note 10).
117 "Anerkennung" (p. 362).
118 Ibid. (p. 363).
119 Ibid. (p. 364).
120 Ibid (p. 363, note 15).
121 Lewis Carroll, "What the Tortoise Said to Achilles."
122 Hare, "Rawls' Theory of Justice" (p. 88). See, however, Stroud's misgivings about this answer in "Inference, Belief, and Understanding" (pp. 190–2).
123 Prichard, "Exchanging" (p. 180).
124 "Anerkennung" (p. 366).
125 *Legitimation Crisis* (p. 104).
126 "Anerkennung" (p. 366).
127 Hare, "The Promising Game" (pp. 151, 155).
128 Ardal, "'And That's a Promise'" (p. 234).
129 It is therefore logical of Ilting to insist on the tautological

character of the principle that agreements must be kept ("Anerkennung," pp. 364f.).

130 Searle, "How to Derive 'Ought' from 'Is,'" first appearing 1964, then revised 1969 in *Speech Acts*.

131 It is doubtful that Hume really asserted Hume's law; see MacIntyre, "Hume on 'Is' and 'Ought.'"

132 Hare, "The Promising Game."

133 James Thomson and Judith Thomson, "How Not to Derive 'Ought' from 'Is.'" The same objection is raised in McClellan and Komisar, "On Deriving 'Ought' from 'Is.'"

134 "The Promising Game" (p. 147).

135 Ibid. (p. 145).

136 Ibid. (p. 149).

137 Ibid. (pp. 149f.). Mackie (*Ethics,* pp. 67f.) and Cooper (*The Diversity of Moral Thinking,* 4.1) argue similarly.

138 *Speech Acts* (pp. 188, 190).

139 Ibid. (pp. 180, 188).

140 Ibid. (p. 181).

141 "How to Derive 'Ought' from 'Is'" (p. 125).

142 "How Not to Derive 'Ought' from 'Is'" (p. 165).

143 Cf. Max Black, "The Gap Between 'Is' and 'Should'" (pp. 101f.).

144 "How Not to Derive 'Ought' from 'Is'" (p. 163). Similarly, McClellan and Komisar, "On Deriving 'Ought' from 'Is'" (p. 158n.).

145 *Speech Acts* (p. 180n.), and recently again: "Prima facie Obligations" (p. 86).

146 Similarly, Hudson's proposal (*The Is–Ought Question,* p. 171). For a discussion of where the clause should be placed, see Narveson, *Morality and Utility* (p. 190, note 35), with reference to Austin, "Other Minds" (p. 102).

147 "The Obligation to Keep a Promise" (p. 169).

148 Ibid. (p. 177).

149 Rawls, *A Theory of Justice* (p. 349); Richards, *A Theory of Reasons for Action* (pp. 166f.).

150 Presumably Hume had this in mind in comparing the inconceivable emergence of a new obligation from a mere act of will to transubstantiation, in *A Treatise of Human Nature* (p. 524).

151 Cf. Anscombe, "Rules, Rights, and Promises"; Atiyah, *Promises, Morals, and Law* (pp. 17f., 128f.); Schelling, "Ethics, Law, and the Exercise of Self-Command" (p. 63).

152 *Prince Friedrich von Homburg* (III, 2).

153 Stephen (*Liberty*, p. 277) can say flatly, "Obligation is simply a metaphor for tying" – as if 'tying' literally described the matter.

154 Wellman, *A Theory of Rights* (p. 28).

155 Thomas Hobbes, *Leviathan* [chap. 17 (the mortal God), chap. 14 (guarantee of contracts)].

156 A point often made in the literature; see, for example, Melden, *Rights and Persons* (p. 32).

157 See Warnock's example in *The Object of Morality* (p. 97).

158 So Ardal describes the example, which indeed came from him ("'And That's a Promise,'" p. 233).

159 See the interesting remarks of a legal scholar on this point: Atiyah, *Promises, Morals, and Law* (pp. 25, 48, 51).

160 In the German edition of this book, I refer here to the word 'verheissen,' current in biblical language, and claim that it differs from 'promise' in that it need not be taken as expressing an obligation to perform the act announced. There is no word in English that corresponds precisely to 'verheissen,' and the relevant biblical passages usually are translated using 'promise' or its cognates; see, e.g., Acts 7:5; 7:17; Rom. 4:13–21; Gal. 3:16–22. But the biblical expressions themselves vary quite a bit on this point. That is to say, sometimes they do suggest an obligation on the part of one who announces, that is, God, and sometimes they do not. Sometimes God is described simply as literally 'having said' to the fathers what he would do, e.g., Gen. 18:19; Lu. 1:55. See the dictionaries of Liddell-Scott and Kittel s.v. 'epangellō.'

161 Atiyah, *Promises, Morals, and Law* (p. 145).

162 Ardal, "'And That's a Promise'"; Narveson, *Morality and Utility* (see the chapter "Incurred Obligations and Duties: Promising as a Paradigm," pp. 185–200); MacCormick, "Voluntary Obligations and Normative Powers."

163 Warnock, *The Object of Morality* (p. 101); Raz, "Voluntary Obligations and Normative Powers" (p. 99).

164 Narveson, *Morality and Utility* (p. 193); see also Atiyah, *Promises, Morals, and Law* (pp. 138–43).

165 Melden, *Rights and Persons* (pp. 44f.).

166 Warnock, *The Object of Morality* (p. 113).

167 Atiyah, *Promises, Morals, and Law* (p. 6), reports a litigation in which the court decided that if the nonfulfillment of a promise did not bring any harm to the recipient of the

promise then that nonfulfillment did not justify any claim by the recipient against the one who made the promise.

168 The understanding I have in mind resembles the 'moral community' Melden appeals to in his account of the obligation arising from promising – except that the community underlying such an understanding is simply not a moral one (Melden, *Rights and Persons,* pp. 44–8).

169 Narveson, *Morality and Utility* (pp. 196f.); Melden, *Rights and Persons* (pp. 48–52).

170 Warnock, *The Object of Morality* (p. 109).

171 Cf. Melden, *Rights and Persons* (pp. 48f.).

172 See Henrich, "Das Problem der Grundlegung der Ethik bei Kant und im spekulativen Idealismus" (pp. 351, 353).

173 See, for example, Gauthier, *Practical Reasoning* (chap. 8); Rawls, *A Theory of Justice* (§3, §40); Wolff, *In Defense of Anarchism;* Wolff, *The Autonomy of Reason;* Czuma, *Autonomie;* Wildt, *Autonomie und Anerkennung;* Prauss, *Kant über Freiheit als Autonomie.* Cf. also the critique of the idea of autonomy in zur Lippe, *Bürgerliche Subjektivität: Autonomie als Selbstzerstörung.*

174 Cf. the "Classification of All Possible Principles of Morality Following from the Assumed Principle of Heteronomy" (GMS 441–443) and the similar table of the material principles of morality in the second *Critique* (*Gesammelte Schriften,* V, p. 40).

175 Ostwald, *Autonomia* (pp. 10, 41). Cf. Bickerman, "Autonomia," and Pohlmann's article in the *Historisches Wörterbuch der Philosophie.*

176 Cf. Kant, *Metaphysik der Sitten* (*Gesammelte Schriften,* VII, p. 318).

177 Kant, *Moral Mrongovius* (*Gesammelte Schriften,* XXVII, p. 1496).

178 Krings, "Freiheit" (p. 501), conflates autonomy and autocracy and so blurs the lines of his own thought; cf. "Freiheit" (pp. 495f., 508). Cf. the reception of this distinction in Benn, "Freedom, Autonomy, and the Concept of a Person."

179 *Du Contrat social* (II, 6).

180 Cf. Beck, *A Commentary on Kant's Critique of Practical Reason* (p. 197).

181 This is Paton's formula III of the categorical imperative, the autonomy formula (*The Categorical Imperative,* XVII, 1).

182 Cf. GMS 400n. and 421n., as well as my essay "Maximen."
183 The phrasing follows GMS 440.
184 See GMS 421, 436.
185 Ameriks, "Kant's Deduction," Section III in particular, interprets this argument against the background of the development of Kant's views on freedom and also points out its weaknesses.
186 Cf. Paton, *The Categorical Imperative* (XXII, 3). An interesting explanation for Kant's surprising diagnosis of circularity is presented in Ameriks, "Kant's Deduction" (III).
187 Henry E. Allison "Morality and Freedom" has developed a noteworthy argument for this proposition, which he calls the 'reciprocity thesis,' and with it he hopes to reconstruct Kant's thought on this matter. The argument: A rational agent must think that her actions can be justified. In particular, she must think that her maxims, owing their validity to her having adopted them, can be justified. But an agent enjoying transcendental freedom cannot justify adopting a maxim by appealing to some given determinant of human nature, for transcendental freedom means independence from all determination by nature. She can justify them only on the grounds of their conformity to the universal and formal rule that Kant calls the unconditional practical law. This is so because, in the case of fundamental maxims, the ground of justification must be such as to hold for all free agents, regardless of their particular desires. The argument is questionable at several points. To mention only the two most serious difficulties: First, even if one grants what is still doubtful, that a rational being must regard his actions as justifiable, it cannot be assumed that these 'actions' also include second-order ones such as that of adopting a maxim for actions; for when people justify their actions, they often do so with reference to their maxims. It is unrealistic to suppose that they always regard these maxims as justifiable in turn. In this way, Allison ascribes to rationality itself a need for 'Letztbegründung' – which all may be very Kantian, but is implausible. Second, assuming the argument did succeed, its result would be considerably weaker than the reciprocity thesis. It still would have to be shown that an unconditional practical law is simply the moral law formulated by Kant in the categorical imperative. Allison does offer a justification for saying this, but he rests it on the following proposition, for which he does not give an argument: An

unconditional practical law, abstracting as it does from all particular desires agents may have, can only require them "to select their maxims on the basis of their suitability as universal laws" (p. 400). But precisely this is questionable (97).

188 Henrich's view of the matter is just the converse: That a free will stands under ethical laws seems unproblematic; important and difficult, on the other hand, is the justification of the claim of the awareness of freedom, in particular by means of the two-worlds doctrine ("Die Deduktion des Sittengesetzes," IX).

189 See Henrich, "Der Begriff der sittlichen Einsicht und Kants Lehre vom Faktum der Vernunft" (p. 245): "The critique of practical reason shows, however, that the validity of the ethical demand for the will analytically follows from the existence of freedom."

190 Cf. my critique of Wolff: "Kausalität aus Freiheit und kategorischer Imperativ" (p. 268).

191 *Kritik der praktischen Vernunft* (*Gesammelte Schriften*, V, p. 27).

192 Ibid. (*Gesammelte Schriften*, V, p. 47).

193 See the discussion in Beck, *A Commentary on Kant's Critique of Practical Reason* (X, 2); Beck, "Das Faktum der Vernunft"; and Henrich, "Der Begriff der sittlichen Einsicht und Kants Lehre von Faktum der Vernunft."

194 *Kritik der praktischen Vernunft* (*Gesammelte Schriften*, V, p.46).

195 Cf. Ilting, "Der naturalistische Fehlschluss bei Kant" (p. 125).

196 Cf. GMS 402, 407, 408, 425, 445, 449f.

197 *Kritik der praktischen Vernunft* (*Gesammelte Schriften*, V, p. 31). Cf. also Kant, *Die Religion innerhalb der Grenzen der blossen Vernunft* (*Gesammelte Schriften*, VI, p. 36).

198 Henrich, "Der Begriff der sittlichen Einsicht" (pp. 227, 247).

199 Ibid. (p. 249).

200 Ameriks, "Kant's Deduction" (IV, V), makes this very clear.

201 Russell, *Introduction to Mathematical Philosophy* (p. 71).

202 Quoted in Henrich, "Der Begriff der sittlichen Einsicht" (p. 235).

203 Hegel, *Phänomenologie des Geistes* (p. 64) (Miller trans., §73).

204 *Kritik der praktischen Vernunft* (*Gesammelte Schriften*, V, p. 29).

205 *A Commentary on Kant's Critique of Practical Reason* (p. 169); "Das Faktum der Vernunft" (p. 280).

206 Cf., for example, Höffe's articles "Begründung" and "Sittlichkeit" in *Lexikon der Ethik* (in particular, pp. 16, 215).

207 On this point, see Henrich, "Das Problem der Grundlegung der Ethik" (pp. 354–6).

208 Hume's point that a sort of transubstantiation is being assumed (*A Treatise of Human Nature*, p. 524) is also pertinent here. Cf. Section 75 in the text and note 150.

209 See, e.g., Rawls, *A Theory of Justice* (§40).

210 Kant italicizes "his" and "something else" in the original text.

211 This point has often been noted; see, e.g., Patzig, "Die logischen Formen praktischer Sätze," and Walker, *Kant* (p. 151).

212 I try to show this in my article "Hypothetische Imperative."

213 For example, Tugendhat writes that the demand of mutual respect applies only to someone "who has taken up the 'must' of moral sanction into his will" ("Retraktationen," p. 164), and Schiller writes in his poem "Das Ideal und das Leben": "Nehmt die Gottheit auf in euren Willen" (Take the divinity up into your will).

214 On this point, see my "Maximen" (pp. 487f.).

215 Cf. the similar statements in the *Kritik der praktischen Vernunft* (*Gesammelte Schriften*, V, p. 32).

216 "Maximen" (pp. 491–3).

217 Cramer, "Hypothetische Imperative?" (pp. 167f.).

218 On the idea overall, cf. my "Maximen" (pp. 486f., 492–4) and, more recently, Höffe, "Kants kategorischer Imperativ" (pp. 87–92). In my paper "Handlungen und Wirkungen," I offered a new analysis of the Kantian sentences quoted earlier and raised doubts about the viability of this concept of action. But these doubts deviate rather far from our ordinary concept of action and seem less plausible than Kant's theory of action in the version given here. That is why I shall not consider them in the present context.

219 Cf. Davidson, "Actions, Reasons and Causes" (p. 182); Hampshire, "Comments on Donald Davidson's 'Intending'" (p. 67); O'Neill, *Acting on Principle* (p. 13).

220 Kant himself describes the will as the faculty of desire, in Section III of the introduction to the *Critique of Judgment*, and also in the first edition of that introduction.

221 Cf. Kenny, *Will, Freedom and Power* (pp. 49–52).
222 Cf. Höffe, "Streben" (p. 1429).
223 Cf. Plato's *Republic* (439c).
224 Schöpf, "Wille" (p. 1720).
225 How the idea of the will as the faculty of desire can mislead is shown by Höffe's statement that will is a "desire that is posited in a relationship to itself" ("Sittlichkeit," p. 1353) – for this is unintelligible.
226 Cf. Bennett, "Action, Reason, and Purpose" (pp. 241–3); Kenny, *Will, Freedom and Power* (p. 21).
227 Cf. Kenny, *Will, Freedom and Power* (p. 21).
228 Cf. ibid. (p. 56).
229 Cf. Thomson, *Acts and Other Events* (pp. 42–6); Bennett, "Action, Reason, and Purpose" (p. 238).
230 Kenny, *Will, Freedom and Power* (p. 53).
231 Ibid. (p. 58).
232 See GMS 431, 432, 433, 434.
233 Cf. GMS 421, 431, 432, 434.
234 See, in particular, GMS 411f.
235 Firth, "Ethical Absolutism and the Ideal Observer."
236 Rawls, *A Theory of Justice* (§3, 4, 24, 30, 40). On this point, cf. Höffe, "Kritische Einführung in Rawls' Theorie der Gerechtigkeit" (p. 188).
237 Habermas, "Vorbereitende Bemerkungen zu einer Theorie der kommunikativen Kompetenz" (pp. 122–41); Apel, "Das Apriori der Kommunikationsgemeinschaft und die Grundlagen der Ethik."
238 Plato, *Republic* (331c).
239 Similarly, Grice, *The Grounds of Moral Judgment* (p. 17).
240 Just two examples: Hospers, "Why Be Moral?" (p. 745), and Richards, *A Theory of Reasons for Action* (p. 282).
241 Cf. Sorabji's considerations in "Aristotle on the Role of Intellect in Virtue" (pp. 202f.); Wiggins, "Deliberation and Practical Reason"; Williams, "Internal and External Reasons" (pp. 104f.).
242 Plato, *Republic* (433a, 519c).
243 Cf. Harman, *Thought* (10.2, 10.4).
244 Neurath, "Protokollsätze" (p. 206).
245 See, e.g., Quine, *Word and Object* (p. 3), and "Natural Kinds" (p. 127).
246 Ross, *The Right and the Good* (p. 28, and often after). Searle first critically discussed the distinction in "Prima facie Obligations."
247 See, e.g., Chisholm, "Practical Reason and the Logic of

Requirement"; Walhout, "Why Should I Be Moral?";
Veatch, "The Rational Justification of Moral Principles":
and, recently, Davis, "Reason, Tradition, Community."

248 On this sense of 'a priori,' cf. *Kritik der reinen Vernunft*, B 2
(*Gesammelte Schriften*, III, p. 28).

249 See von Wright, *The Varieties of Goodness* (V); Kenny,
"Happiness"; Hammacher, "Glück"; Hinske, "Zwischen
fortuna und felicitas"; and the volume edited by Bien: *Die
Frage nach dem Glück.*

250 *Nicomachean Ethics* (NE) (1095a19f.).

251 The tradition rests on the first chapter of the *Nicomachean
Ethics*. For extensive discussion of this text, cf. de Vogel,
"Quelques remarques à propos du premier chapitre de
l'EN"; Ackrill, "Aristotle on Eudaimonia"; and Jacobi,
"Aristoteles' Einführung des Begriffs 'eudaimonia' im I.
Buch der 'Nikomachischen Ethik.'"

252 On this point, cf. again Kant, GMS 418.

253 But see Gauthier and Jolif's protest against the French
translation of 'phronēsis' by 'prudence,' which they recommend replacing by 'sagesse' (*Commentaire*, p. 463).

254 No such history of the concept exists. Some indications
are made in F. Wiedmann and G. Biller's article in *Historisches Wörterbuch der Philosophie.*

255 NE (1140a24–28) (my translation); see also NE (1141b9–
14).

256 Thomas Aquinas, *Summa theologica* (II, II, 47); Pieper, *Das
Viergespann* (p. 15).

257 NE (1144b16f.).

258 See Forschner's objection to my account here in his review
of the German edition of this book.

259 NE (1141b8 with 1112b11, 1144a8); on the other hand,
NE (1141b15, 1142b33). Cf. Gadamer, *Wahrheit und Methode* (pp. 304f.) (trans., pp. 286f.); J. Cooper, *Reason and
Human Good in Aristotle* (I, 2–4); Wiggins, "Deliberation
and Practical Reason."

260 See Wilkes, "The Good Man and the Good for Man in
Aristotle's Ethics" (in particular, pp. 566f.). Cf. J. Cooper,
Reason and Human Good in Aristotle (II, 2–5).

261 NE (1144b27f.).

262 GMS 418; see Section 149 in the text.

263 *Der Streit der Fakultäten*, part 3: "Von der Macht des
Gemüts, durch den blossen Vorsatz seiner krankhaften
Gefühle Meister zu sein" (*Gesammelte Schriften*, VII, p.
99).

264 *Republic* (444d–e) (Cornford's translation).

265 Kant, *Kritik der praktischen Vernunft* (V, p. 20).

266 Patzig's example ("Die logischen Formen praktischer Sätze in Kants Ethik," p. 107).

267 Aristotle explicitly mentions calculation ('logismos') on the part of the prudent man (NE, 1141b14).

268 Cf. again Aristotle, NE (1141b14–16).

269 Gauthier's treatise also proceeds from cases of this kind as examples of practical problems (*Practical Reasoning,* p. 1).

270 A similar idea can be found in Harman, "Practical Reasoning"; he does not specifically refer to prudence, however.

271 Mabbott, "Prudence" (pp. 54f., 61).

272 Ibid. (p. 56).

273 Ibid. (p. 55).

274 Ibid. (pp. 61, 62f.).

275 Horsburgh disputes this in his comments on Mabbott's paper ("Prudence," pp. 72, 73, 75, 76).

276 Hobbes, *Leviathan* (chap. 17).

277 Henrich, "Die Deduktion des Sittengesetzes" (X).

278 Foot, "Reasons for Action and Desires" (p. 156).

279 Foot, introduction to *Virtues and Vices* (p. xiv).

280 Foot, "Morality as a System of Hypothetical Imperatives" (p. 167).

281 Ibid. (p. 166).

282 Foot, "A Reply to Professor Frankena" (p. 174), and p. xiv of the introduction to *Virtues and Vices.*

283 Tugendhat ("Retraktationen," pp. 143f.) displays similar misgivings regarding Wolf, *Das Problem des moralischen Sollens.* Wilkes's interpretation of Aristotle ("The Good Man and the Good for Man") suffers from what substantially is the same difficulty. Bernard Williams's encouraging assurance – "A respect for freedom and social justice and a critique of oppressive and deceitful institutions . . . we need not suppose that we have no ideas to give them a basis" (*Ethics and the Limits of Philosophy,* p. 198) – leaves one wondering what this basis is supposed to be.

284 Foot, "Morality as a System of Hypothetical Imperatives" (p. 169).

285 Cf. again Foot, "Morality as a System of Hypothetical Imperatives" (p. 170).

286 Cf. Henrich, "Das Problem der Grundlegung der Ethik bei Kant und im spekulativen Idealismus" (p. 386).

287 Odo Marquard, "Hegel und das Sollen," gives a different reading.

288 That is, Hegel, *Phänomenologie des Geistes* (PhG) (Hoff-meister ed., pp. 285–301) (Miller trans., *Phenomenology of Spirit*, §397–418, and accordingly in the following).

289 "Wissenschaft der Erfahrung des Bewusstseins" (*Phänomenologie*, Hoffmeister ed., p. xxx); not included in Miller's translation. Some copies of the original edition contain a page with this title; others do not. Cf. Nicolin, "Zum Titelproblem der *Phänomenologie des Geistes*."

290 Hegel himself (PhG 75/89) draws attention to this turning point in the book; cf. Pöggeler, "Die Komposition der *Phänomenologie des Geistes*" (pp. 44–6).

291 Heidegger, *Sein und Zeit* (p. 11) (Macquarrie and Robinson trans., p. 32).

292 Heidegger explains this in *Kant und das Problem der Metaphysik* (pp. 206–8).

293 Schiller, *Wallenstein's Death* (I, 4).

294 Cf. Marx, "Ökonomische-philosophische Manuskripte" (p. 599) (*Marx-Engels Reader*, p. 87).

295 Goethe's poem "Dauer im Wechsel" gives a picture of this turn.

296 Aubenque, *La prudence chez Aristote,* interprets Aristotelian 'phronēsis' in this sense; 'phronēsis' is the property of being mindful of mortality.

297 On this, see, above all, Fulda, *Das Problem einer Einleitung in Hegels Wissenschaft der Logik.*

298 Hegel, *Logik* (I, p. 145) (Miller trans., *Logic*, I, p. 154).

299 Cf. Theunissen, *Sein und Schein* (pp. 267–97).

300 That is, Hegel, *Wissenschaft der Logik* (I, pp. 116f.) (Miller trans., *Science of Logic,* p. 129; and accordingly in the following).

301 *Pensées* (434, Brunschvicg's numeration). Cf., however, Montaigne, *Essais* (II, 12), penultimate paragraph, which in turn refers to Seneca's preface to the first book of *Naturales quaestiones.*

302 Cf. Plato, *Republic* (479b,d).

303 Cf. Theunissen, *Sein und Schein* (pp. 279–82).

304 "In younger days I was glad of morning, / At evening I wept; now that I am older, / I begin my day in doubt, yet / Holy and bright to me is its end."

Bibliography

Ackrill, J. L. "Aristotle on Eudaimonia" (first published 1974). In *Essays on Aristotle's Ethics,* edited by A. Rorty, pp. 15–33. Berkeley, 1980.

Adams, E. M. "Gewirth on Reason and Morality." *Review of Metaphysics* 33 (1980), 579–92.

Aiken, Henry David. "The Concept of Moral Objectivity." In *Morality and the Language of Conduct,* edited by H. Castañeda and G. Nakhnikian, pp. 69–105. Detroit, 1963.

Allison, Henry E. "Morality and Freedom: Kant's Reciprocity Thesis." *Philosophical Review* 95 (1986), 393–425.

Ameriks, Karl. "Kant's Deduction of Freedom and Morality." *Journal of the History of Philosophy* 19 (1981), 53–79.

Angehrn, Emil. *Freiheit und System bei Hegel.* Berlin and New York, 1977.

Anscombe, G. E. M. "Modern Moral Philosophy." *Philosophy* 33 (1958), 1–19.

Intention. Oxford, 1972.

"Rules, Rights, and Promises." *Midwest Studies in Philosophy* 3 (1978), 318–23.

Apel, Karl Otto. "Das Apriori der Kommunikationsgemeinschaft und die Grundlagen der Ethik." In Apel, K. O., *Transformation der Philosophie,* vol. 2, pp. 358–435. Frankfurt a.M., 1973.

"Lässt sich ethische Vernunft von strategischer Zweckrationalität unterscheiden? Zum Problem der Rationalität sozialer Kommunikation und Interaktion." *Archivo di filosofia* 51 (1983), 375–434.

"The Question of the Rationality of Social Interaction." In *Philosophy and Science in Phenomenological Perspective,* edited by K. K. Cho, pp. 9–29. Loewen, 1984.

Ardal, Pall S. "'And That's a Promise.'" *Philosophical Quarterly* 18 (1968), 225–37.

Aristotle. *The Nicomachean Ethics,* trans. Martin Ostwald. Indianapolis, 1962.

Atiyah, P. S. *Promises, Morals, and Law.* Oxford, 1981.

Aubenque, Pierre. *La prudence chez Aristote.* Paris, 1963.

Austin, J. L. "Other Minds" (first published 1946). In *Philosophical Papers,* edited by J. O. Urmson and G. J. Warnock. Oxford, 1969.

Baier, Kurt. *The Moral Point of View: A Rational Basis for Ethics.* Ithaca, 1958.

"Moral Reasons and Reasons to Be Moral." In *Values and Morals,* edited by A. Goldman and J. Kim, pp. 231–56. Dordrecht, 1978.

Baum, Manfred, and Meist, Kurt. "Durch Philosophie Leben Lernen. Hegels Konzeption der Philosophie nach den neuaufgefundenen Jenaer Manuskripten." *Hegel-Studien* 12 (1977), 32–81.

Baumeister, Thomas. *Hegels frühe Kritik an Kants Ethik.* Heidelberg, 1976.

Bayles, Michael D. "Singer's Moral Principles and Rules." *Philosophical Studies* 16 (1965), 61–4.

Beck, Lewis White. "Das Faktum der Vernunft. Zur Rechtfertigungsproblematik in der Ethik." *Kant-Studien* 52 (1960–1), 271–82.

A Commentary on Kant's Critique of Practical Reason. Chicago, 1960.

Becker, Lawrence. *On Justifying Moral Judgments.* London, 1973.

Benn, S. I. "Freedom, Autonomy, and the Concept of a Person." *Proceedings of the Aristotelian Society* 76 (1976), 109–30.

Bennett, Daniel. "Action, Reason, and Purpose" (first published 1965). In *Readings in the Theory of Action,* edited by N. Care and C. Landesman, pp. 238–52. Bloomington, 1968.

Bickerman, E. J. "Autonomia. Sur un passage de Thucydide (1.144, 2)." *Revue internationale des droits de l'antiquité* 5 (1958), 313–44.

Bien, Günther (ed.). *Die Frage nach dem Glück.* Stuttgart, 1978.

Bitsch, Brigitte. *Sollensbegriff und Moralitätskritik bei G. W. F. Hegel: Interpretationen zur 'Wissenschaft der Logik,' 'Phänomenologie,' und 'Rechtsphilosophie.'* Bonn, 1977.

Bittner, Rüdiger. "Maximen." In *Akten des 4. Internationaen Kant-Kongesses,* edited by G. Funke, pp. 485–98. Mainz, 1974.

"Kausalität aus Freiheit und kategorischer Imperativ." *Zeitschrift für philosophische Forschung* 32 (1978), 265–74.

"Hypothetische Imperative." *Zeitschrift für philosophische Forschung* 34 (1980), 210–26.

"Thomas Hobbes' Staatskonstruktion – Verunft und Gewalt." *Zeitschrift für philosophische Forschung* 37 (1983), 389–403.

"Handlungen und Wirkungen." In *Handlungstheorie und Transzendentalphilosophie,* edited by G. Prauss, pp. 13–26. Frankfurt a.M., 1986.

Black, Max. "The Gap Between 'Is' and 'Should'" (first published 1964). In *The Is–Ought Question,* edited by W. D. Hudson, pp. 99–113. London, 1969.

Bradley, F. H. *Ethical Studies* (2nd ed.; first published 1876). Oxford, 1927.

Brock, Dan W. "The Justification of Morality." *American Philosophical Quarterly* 14 (1977), 71–8.

Carnap, Rudolf. "Empiricism, Semantics and Ontology" (first published 1950). In *Semantics and the Philosophy of Language,* edited by L. Linsky, pp. 208–30. Urbana, 1952.

Carroll, Lewis. "What the Tortoise Said to Achilles." *Mind* 4 (1895), 278–80.

Chisholm, Roderick. "Practical Reason and the Logic of Requirement" (first published 1974). In *Practical Reasoning,* edited by J. Raz, pp. 118–27. Oxford, 1978.

Cooper, John M. *Reason and Human Good in Aristotle.* Cambridge, Mass., 1975.

Cooper, Neil. *The Diversity of Moral Thinking.* Oxford, 1981.

Craemer-Ruegenberg, Ingrid. *Moralsprache und Moralität. Zu Thesen der sprachanalytischen Ethik.* Freiburg and Munich, 1975.

Cramer, Konrad. "Hypothetische Imperative?" In *Rehabilitierung der praktischen Philosophie,* vol. 1, edited by M. Riedel, pp. 159–212. Freiburg i.Br., 1972.

Czuma, Hans. *Autonomie. Eine hypothetische Konstruktion praktischer Vernunft.* Freiburg and Munich, 1974.

Darwall, Stephen L. *Impartial Reason.* Ithaca, 1983.

Davidson, Donald. "Actions, Reasons and Causes" (first published 1963). In *Readings in the Theory of Action,* edited by N. Care and C. Landesman, pp. 179–89. Bloomington, 1968.

"On the Very Idea of a Conceptual Scheme." *Proceedings of the American Philosophical Association* 48 (1974), 5–20.

"Intending." In *Philosophy of History and Action,* edited by Y. Yovel, pp. 41–60. Dordrecht, 1978.

Davis, Charles. "Reason, Tradition, Community: The Search for Ethical Foundations." In *Foundations of Ethics,* edited by C. Rouner, pp. 37–56. Notre Dame, 1983.

Diggs, B. J. "Review of Grice." *Philosophical Review* 78 (1969), 543–6.

Dworkin, Ronald. "The Original Position" (first published

1973). In *Reading Rawls. Critical Studies on Rawls' "A Theory of Justice,"* edited by N. Daniels, pp. 16–53. Oxford, 1975.

Ellscheid, Günther. *Das Problem von Sein und Sollen in der Philosophie Immanuel Kants.* Cologne, 1968.

Ezorsky, Gertrude. "Ad Hominem Morality." *Journal of Philosophy* 63 (1966), 120–5.

Fahrenbach, Helmut. "Ein programmatischer Aufriss der Problemlage und systematischen Ansatzmöglichkeiten praktischer Philosophie." In *Rehabilitierung der praktischen Philosophie,* vol. 1, edited by M. Riedel, pp. 15–56. Freiburg i.Br., 1972.

Falk, W. D. "Morality, Self and Others." In *Morality and the Language of Conduct,* edited by H. Castañeda and G. Nakhnikian, pp. 25–67. Detroit, 1963.

Firth, Roderick. "Ethical Absolutism and the Ideal Observer" (first published 1952). In *Readings in Ethical Theory,* edited by W. Sellars and J. Hospers, pp. 200–21. New York, 1970.

Fischer, D. R. "Why Should I Be Just?" *Proceedings of the Aristotelian Society* 77 (1976–7), 43–61.

Foot, Philippa. "Moral Beliefs" (first published 1958). In *Virtues and Vices,* pp. 110–31. Oxford, 1978.

"Moral Arguments" (first published 1958). In *Virtues and Vices,* pp. 96–109. Oxford, 1978.

"Morality as a System of Hypothetical Imperatives" (first published 1972). In *Virtues and Vices,* pp. 157–73. Oxford, 1978.

"Reasons for Actions and Desires" (first published 1972). In *Virtues and Vices,* pp. 148–56. Oxford, 1978.

"Reply to Professor Frankena" (first published 1975). In *Virtues and Vices,* pp. 174–80. Oxford, 1978.

Virtues and Vices and Other Essays in Moral Philosophy. Oxford, 1978.

Forschner, Maximilian. *Gesetz und Freiheit. Zum Problem der Autonomie bei Immanuel Kant.* Munich and Salzburg, 1974.

"Klugheit versus Moralität" (review of the German first edition of the present book). *Zeitschrift für philosophische Forschung* 39 (1985), 600–8.

Frankena, W. K. "The Naturalistic Fallacy" (first published 1939). In *Readings in Ethical Theory,* edited by W. Sellars and J. Hospers, pp. 103–14. New York, 1970.

"Obligation and Motivation in Recent Moral Philosophy" (first published 1958). In *Readings in Ethical Theory,* edited by W. Sellars and J. Hospers, pp. 708–29. New York, 1970.

Ethics. Englewood Cliffs, N.J., 1963.

"Recent Conceptions of Morality." In *Morality and the Language of Conduct,* edited by H. Castañeda and G. Nakhnikian, pp. 1–24. Detroit, 1963.

"The Concept of Morality." *Journal of Philosophy* 63 (1966), 688–96.

Fulda, H. F. *Das Problem einer Einleitung in Hegels Wissenschaft der Logik.* Frankfurt a.M., 1965.

Gadamer, Hans-Georg. *Wahrheit und Methode. Grundzüge einer philosophischen Hermeneutik.* Tübingen, 1960 (trans.: *Truth and Method.* New York, 1975).

"Über die Möglichkeit einer philosophischen Ethik." In *Sein und Ethos. Untersuchungen zur Grundlegung der Ethik,* edited by P. Engelhardt, pp. 11–24. Mainz, 1963.

Gauthier, David P. *Practical Reasoning. The Structure and Foundations of Prudential and Moral Arguments and Their Exemplification in Discourse.* Oxford, 1963.

"Morality and Advantage" (first published 1967). In *Practical Reasoning,* edited by J. Raz, pp. 185–97. Oxford, 1978.

"Reason and Maximization." *Canadian Journal of Philosophy* 4 (1975), 411–33.

Gauthier, R. A., and Jolif, J. Y. *Aristote, L'Ethique à Nicomaque. Introduction, traduction et commentaire,* 2 vols. Louvain and Paris, 1958–9.

Gewirth, Alan. "Must One Play the Moral Language Game?" *American Philosophical Quarterly* 7 (1970), 107–18.

Reason and Morality. Chicago, 1978.

Gigon, Olof. "Phronesis und Sophia in der Nikomachischen Ethik des Aristoteles." In *Kephalaion. Studies in Greek Philosophy and Its Continuation. Offered to C. J. de Vogel,* edited by J. Mansfeld et al. Assen, 1975.

Görland, Ingtraud. *Die Kantkritik des jungen Hegel.* Frankfurt a.M., 1966.

Grewendorf, Günther, and Meggle, Georg (eds.). *Seminar: Sprache und Ethik. Zur Entwicklung der Metaethik.* Frankfurt a.M., 1974.

Grice, Geoffrey Russell. *The Grounds of Moral Judgment.* Cambridge, U.K. 1967.

Griffiths, A. Phillips. "Justifying Moral Principles." *Proceedings of the Aristotelian Society* 58 (1957–8), 103–24.

"Ultimate Moral Principles: Their Justification." In *Encyclopedia of Philosophy,* vol. 8, edited by P. Edwards, pp. 176–82. New York, 1967.

Griffiths, A. P[hillips], and Peters, R. S. "The Autonomy of Prudence." *Mind* 71 (1962), 161–80.

Habermas, Jürgen. "Vorbereitende Bemerkungen zu einer Theorie der kommunikativen Kompetenz." In *Theorie der Gesellschaft oder Sozialtechnologie*, edited by J. Habermas and N. Luhmann, pp. 101–141. Frankfurt a.M., 1971.

Legitimationsprobleme im Spätkapitalismus. Frankfurt a.M., 1973 (trans.: *Legitimation Crisis*, trans. Thomas McCarthy, Boston, 1975).

"Wahrheitstheorien." In *Wirklichkeit und Reflexion*, edited by H. Fahrenbach, pp. 211–65. Pfullingen, 1973.

"Zwei Bemerkungen zum praktischen Diskurs." In *Zur Rekonstruktion des historischen Materialismus*, edited by J. Habermas, pp. 338–46. Frankfurt a.M., 1976.

"Diskursethik – Notizen zu einem Begründungsprogramm." In *Moralbewusstsein und kommunikatives Handeln*, edited by J. Habermas, pp. 53–125. Frankfurt a.M., 1983.

Hammacher, Klaus. "Glück." In *Handbuch philosophischer Grundbegriffe*, vol. 2, edited by H. Krings, H. M. Baumgartner, and C. Wild, pp. 606–14. Munich, 1973.

Hampshire, Stuart. "Comments on Donald Davidson's 'Intending.'" In *Philosophy of History and Action*, edited by Y. Yovel, pp. 61–8. Dordrecht, 1978.

Hardie, W. F. R. *Aristotle's Ethical Theory*. Oxford, 1968.

"Aristotle on the Best Life for a Man." *Philosophy* 54 (1979), 35–50.

Hare, R. M. *The Language of Morals*. Oxford, 1952.

Freedom and Reason. Oxford, 1963.

"The Promising Game" (first published 1964). In *The Is–Ought Question*, edited by W. D. Hudson, pp. 144–56. London, 1969.

"Review of Warnock." *Ratio* 14 (1972), 193–200.

"Rawls' Theory of Justice" (first published 1973). In *Reading Rawls: Critical Studies on Rawls' "A Theory of Justice,"* edited by N. Daniels, pp. 81–107. Oxford, 1975.

Harman, Gilbert. *Thought*. Princeton, 1973.

"Practical Reasoning." *Review of Metaphysics* 29 (1975–6), 431–63.

The Nature of Morality. Oxford, 1977.

Harrison, Jonathan. "When Is a Principle a Moral Principle?" *Proceedings of the Aristotelian Society, Suppl.* 28 (1954), 111–34.

"Moral Scepticism." *Proceedings of the Aristotelian Society, Suppl.* 41 (1967), 199–214.

Hegel, Georg Wilhelm Friedrich. *Phänomenologie des Geistes* (first published 1807), edited by J. Hoffmeister. Hamburg, 1952 (trans.: *Phenomenology of Spirit*, trans. A. V. Miller, Oxford, 1977).

Wissenschaft der Logik, vol. 1 (first published 1812), edited by G. Lasson. Hamburg, 1963 (trans.: *Hegel's Science of Logic*, trans. A. V. Miller, London and New York, 1969).

Gesammelte Werke, vol. 5, edited by M. Baum and K. R. Meist. Hamburg, to appear.

Heidegger, Martin. *Sein und Zeit*. Tübingen, 1963 (trans.: *Being and Time*, trans. John Macquarrie and Edward Robinson, London, 1962).

Kant und das Problem der Metaphysik. Frankfurt a.M., 1965.

Henrich, Dieter. "Der Begriff der sittlichen Einsicht und Kants Lehre vom Faktum der Vernunft" (first published 1960). In *Kant: Zur Deutung seiner Theorie von Erkennen und Handeln*, edited by G. Prauss, pp. 223–54. Cologne, 1973.

"Das Problem der Grundlegung der Ethik bei Kant und im spekulativen Idealismus." In *Sein und Ethos*, edited by P. Engelhardt, pp. 350–86. Mainz, 1963.

"Die Deduktion des Sittengesetzes. Über die Gründe der Dunkelheit des letzten Abschnittes von Kants 'Grundlegung zur Metaphysik der Sitten.'" In *Denken im Schatten des Nihilismus: Festschrift für Wilhelm Weischedel*, edited by A. Schwan, pp. 55–112. Darmstadt, 1975.

Hinske, Norbert. "Zwischen fortuna und felicitas: Glücksvorstellungen im Wandel der Zeiten." *Philosophisches Jahrbuch* 85 (1978), 317–30.

Höffe, Otfried. *Praktische Philosophie. Das Modell des Aristoteles*. Munich, 1970.

"Sittlichkeit." In *Handbuch philosophischer Grundbegriffe*, vol. 3, edited by H. Krings, H. M. Baumgartner, and C. Wild, pp. 1341–58. Munich, 1974.

"Streben." In *Handbuch philosophischer Grundbegriffe*, vol. 3, edited by H. Krings, H. M. Baumgartner, and C. Wild, pp. 1419–30. Munich, 1974.

Strategien der Humanität. Zur Ethik öffentlicher Entscheidungsprozesse. Munich, 1975.

"Grundaussagen über den Menschen bei Aristoteles" (first published 1976). In *Ethik und Politik*, pp. 13–37. Frankfurt a.M., 1979.

"Kants kategorischer Imperativ als Kriterium des Sittlichen" (first published 1977). In *Ethik und Politik*, pp. 84–119. Frankfurt a.M., 1979.

"Kritische Einführung in Rawls' Theorie der Gerechtigkeit" (first published 1977). In *Ethik und Politik*, pp. 160–94. Frankfurt a.M., 1979.

"Begründung." In *Lexikon der Ethik*, edited by O. Höffe, pp. 15–17. Munich, 1977.

"Sittlichkeit." In *Lexikon der Ethik*, edited by O. Höffe, pp. 213–16. Munich, 1977.

"Zur vertragstheoretischen Begründung politischer Gerechtigkeit: Hobbes, Kant und Rawls im Vergleich." In *Ethik und Politik*, pp. 195–226. Frankfurt a.M., 1979.

Ethik und Politik: Grundmodelle und -probleme der praktischen Philosophie. Frankfurt a.M., 1979.

Holland, R. "Moral Scepticism." *Proceedings of the Aristotelian Society, Suppl.* 41 (1967), 185–98.

Horsburgh, H. J. N. "Prudence." *Proceedings of the Aristotelian Society, Suppl.* 36 (1962), 65–76.

Hospers, John. "Why Be Moral?" (first published 1961). In *Readings in Ethical Theory*, edited by W. Sellars and J. Hospers, pp. 730–46. New York, 1970.

Hudson, W. D. (ed.). *The Is-Ought Question: A Collection of Papers on the Central Problem in Moral Philosophy*. London, 1969.

Hume, David. *A Treatise of Human Nature*, edited by A. Selby-Bigge. Oxford, 1888.

Ilting, Karl-Heinz. "Der naturalistische Fehlschluss bei Kant." In *Rehabilitierung der praktischen Philosophie*, vol. 1, edited by M. Riedel, pp. 113–30. Freiburg i.Br., 1972.

"Anerkennung: Zur Rechtfertigung praktischer Sätze." In *Rehabilitierung der praktischen Philosophie*, vol. 2, edited by M. Riedel, pp. 353–68. Freiburg i.Br., 1974.

Jackson, Reginald. "Practical Reason." *Philosophy* 17 (1942), 351–67.

Jacobi, Klaus. "Aristoteles' Einführung des Begriffs 'eudaimonia' im I. Buch der 'Nikomachischen Ethik.' Eine Antwort auf einige neuere Inkonsistenzkritiken." *Philosophisches Jahrbuch* 86 (1979), 300–25.

Kambartel, Friedrich (ed.). *Praktische Philosophie und konstruktive Wissenschaftstheorie*. Frankfurt a.M., 1974.

"Wie ist praktische Philosophie konstruktiv möglich? Über einige Missverständnisse eines methodischen Verständnisses praktischer Diskurse." In *Praktische Philosophie und konstruktive Wissenschaftstheorie*, pp. 9–33. Frankfurt a.M., 1974.

"Letter to Lorenzen." In *Praktische Philosophie und konstruktive Wissenschaftstheorie*, pp. 232–3. Frankfurt a.M., 1974.

"Letter to Schwemmer." In *Praktische Philosophie und konstruktive Wissenschaftstheorie*, pp. 234–5. Frankfurt a.M., 1974.

Kant, Immanuel. *Gesammelte Schriften* (ed. Königliche preussische Akademie der Wissenschaften). Berlin, 1910 et seq.

Critique of Practical Reason, trans. Lewis W. Beck. New York, 1956.

Foundations of the Metaphysics of Morals, trans. Lewis W. Beck. New York, 1959.

Kekes, John. "Moral Conventionalism." *American Philosophical Quarterly* 22 (1985), 37–46.

Kenny, Anthony. "Happiness" (first published 1965–6). In *Moral Concepts*, edited by J. Feinberg, pp. 43–52. Oxford, 1969.

Action, Emotion and Will. London, 1969.

Will, Freedom and Power. Oxford, 1975.

Körner, Stephan. "The Impossibility of Transcendental Deductions." *The Monist* 51 (1967), 317–31.

Krings, Hermann. "Freiheit." In *Handbuch philosophischer Grundbegriffe*, vol. 1, edited by H. Krings, H. M. Baumgartner, and C. Wild, pp. 493–510. Munich, 1973.

"Empirie und Apriori. Zum Verhältnis von Transzendentalphilosophie und Sprachpragmatik." *Neue Hefte für Philosophie* 14 (1978), 57–75.

Kuhlmann, Wolfgang. "Zur logischen Struktur transzendentalpragmatischer Normenbegründungen." In *Transzendentalphilosophische Normenbegründungen*, edited by W. Oelmüller, pp. 15–26. Paderborn, 1978.

"Reflexive Letztbegründung. Zur These von der Unhintergehbarkeit der Argumentationssituation." *Zeitschrift für philosophische Forschung* 35 (1981), 3–26.

Kupperman, Joel. *The Foundations of Morality*. London, 1983.

Lippe, Rudolf zur. *Bürgerliche Subjektivität: Autonomie als Selbstzerstörung*. Frankfurt a.M., 1975.

Lorenzen, Paul. *Normative Logic and Ethics*. Mannheim, 1969.

"Szientismus versus Dialektik." In *Hermeneutik und Dialektik*, vol. 1, edited by R. Bubner, K. Cramer, and R. Wiehl, pp. 57–72. Tübingen, 1970.

"Letter to Kambartel." In *Praktische Philosophie und konstruktive Wissenschaftstheorie*, edited by F. Kambartel, pp. 225–7. Frankfurt a.M., 1974.

Lorenzen, Paul, and Schwemmer, Oswald. *Konstruktive Logik, Ethik und Wissenschaftstheorie*. Mannheim, 1973.

Mabbott, J. D. "Prudence." *Proceedings of the Aristotelian Society,
Suppl.* 36 (1962), 51–64.

McClellan, J. E., and Komisar, B. P. "On Deriving 'Ought'
from 'Is'" (first published 1964). In *The Is-Ought Question,*
edited by W. D. Hudson, pp. 157–62. London, 1969.

MacCormick, Neil. "Voluntary Obligations and Normative
Powers." *Proceedings of the Aristotelian Society, Suppl.* 46
(1972), 59–78.

McDowell, John. "Are Moral Requirements Hypothetical Imperatives?" *Proceedings of the Aristotelian Society, Suppl.* 52
(1978), 12–29.

"The Role of Eudaimonia in Aristotle's Ethics" (first published 1980). In *Essays on Aristotle's Ethics,* edited by A.
Rorty, pp. 359–76. Berkeley, 1980.

McGuiness, B. F. "'I Know What I Want.'" *Proceedings of the
Aristotelian Society* 57 (1956–7), 305–20.

McIntyre, Alasdair. "Hume on 'Is' and 'Ought.'" *Philosophical
Review* 68 (1959), 451–68.

"Imperatives, Reasons for Action and Morals." *Journal of Philosophy* 62 (1965), 513–24.

After Virtue: A Study in Moral Theory. Notre Dame, 1981.

Mackie, John. *Ethics: Inventing Right and Wrong.* Harmonds-
worth, 1977.

Marquard, Odo. "Hegel und das Sollen." *Philosophisches Jahrbuch* 72 (1964–5), 103–19.

Marx, Karl. "Ökonomisch-philosophische Manuskripte
(1844)." In *Frühe Schriften,* vol. 1, edited by H. J. Lieber and
P. Furth, Darmstadt, 1971 (trans.: "The Economic and Philosophical Manuscripts of 1844." In *The Marx-Engels Reader,* edited by Robert Tucker, pp. 66–125. New York,
1978).

Meerbote, Ralf. "Kant on Freedom and the Rational and Morally Good Will." In *Self and Nature in Kant's Philosophy,* edited
by A. Wood, pp. 57–72. Ithaca, 1984.

Melden, A. I. "Why Be Moral?" *Journal of Philosophy* 45 (1948),
449–56.

"On Promising." *Mind* 65 (1956), 49–66.

Free Action. London, 1961.

Rights and Persons. Oxford, 1977.

Mitchell, Dorothy. "Warum soll ich sittlich sein?" *Ratio* 12
(1970), 120–4.

Monro, D. H. "Critical Notice on Kurt Baier, *The Moral Point
of View.*" *Australasian Journal of Philosophy* 37 (1959), 71–8.

Nagel, Thomas. *The Possibility of Altruism*. Oxford, 1970.
The View from Nowhere. New York, 1986.

Narveson, Jan. *Morality and Utility*. Baltimore, 1967.
"Review of Warnock." *Mind* 81 (1972), 288–99.

Neurath, Otto. "Protokollsätze." *Erkenntnis* 3 (1932–3), 204–14.

Nicolin, Friedhelm. "Zum Titelproblem der *Phänomenologie des Geistes*." *Hegel-Studien* 4 (1967), 113–23.

Nielsen, Kai. "Is 'Why Should I Be Moral?' an Absurdity?" *Australasian Journal of Philosophy* 36 (1958), 25–32.
"Why Should I Be Moral?" (first published 1963). In *Readings in Ethical Theory*, edited by W. Sellars and J. Hospers, pp. 747–68. New York, 1970.
"On Being Moral." *Philosophical Studies* 16 (1965), 1–4.
" 'Why Should I Be Moral?' Revisited." *American Philosophical Quarterly* 21 (1984), 81–91.

Norman, Richard. *Reasons for Actions*. Oxford, 1971.

Oelmüller, Willi (ed.). *Transzendentalphilosophische Normenbegründungen*. Paderborn, 1978.

O'Neill, Onora. *Acting on Principle: An Essay on Kantian Ethics*. New York, 1975.

Ostwald, Martin. *Autonomia: Its Genesis and Early History* (American Classical Studies 11). Chico, Calif., 1982.

Paton, H. J. *The Good Will: A Study in the Coherence Theory of Goodness*. London, 1927.
The Categorical Imperative. A Study in Kant's Moral Philosophy. New York, 1965.

Patzig, Günther. "Die logischen Formen praktischer Sätze in Kants Ethik" (first published 1966). In Patzig, *Ethik ohne Metaphysik*, pp. 101–26. Göttingen, 1971.
"Review of John Rawls' *A Theory of Justice*." *Allgemeine Zeitschrift für Philosophie* 1 (1976), 62–5.

Peters, R. S. *The Concept of Motivation*. London, 1960.

Phillips, D. Z. "Does It Pay to Be Good?" *Proceedings of the Aristotelian Society* 65 (1964–5), 45–60.
"In Search of the Moral 'Must.' Mrs. Foot's Fugitive Thought." *Philosophical Quarterly* 27 (1977), 140–57.

Pieper, Joseph. *Das Viergespann: Klugheit, Tapferkeit, Gerechtigkeit, Mass*. Munich, 1964.

Plato, *Republic*, trans. Francis M. Cornford. Oxford, 1971.

Pöggeler, Otto. "Die Komposition der *Phänomenologie des Geistes*." *Hegel-Studien, Suppl*. 3 (1966), 27–47.

Pohlmann, R. "Autonomie." In *Historisches Wörterbuch der Philo-*

sophie, vol. 1, edited by J. Ritter, columns 701–19. Darmstadt, 1971.

Prauss, Gerold. *Kant über Freiheit als Autonomie.* Frankfurt a.M., 1983.

Prichard, H. A. "The Obligation to Keep a Promise." In Prichard *Moral Obligation,* pp. 169–79. Oxford, 1949.

"Exchanging." In *Moral Obligation,* pp. 180–1. Oxford, 1949.

Quine, Willard V. O. *Word and Object.* Cambridge, Mass., 1960.

"Natural Kinds." In Quine, *Ontological Relativity and Other Essays,* pp. 114–38. New York, 1969.

Ralls, Anthony. "The Game of Life." *Philosophical Quarterly* 16 (1966), 23–4.

Rawls, John. *A Theory of Justice.* Oxford, 1972.

Raz, Joseph. "Voluntary Obligations and Normative Powers." *Proceedings of the Aristotelian Society, Suppl.* 46 (1972), 79–102.

Practical Reason and Norms. London, 1975.

(ed.). *Practical Reasoning.* Oxford, 1978.

Reibenschuh, Gernot. "Warum moralisch sein? Zur Kritik soziologischer Moralbegründung." In *Rehabilitierung der praktischen Philosophie,* vol. 2, edited by M. Riedel, pp. 85–118. Freiburg i.Br., 1974.

Richards, David A. J. *A Theory of Reasons for Action.* Oxford, 1971.

Riedel, Manfred (ed.). *Rehabilitierung der praktischen Philosophie,* vol. 1: *Geschichte, Probleme, Aufgaben.* Freiburg i.Br., 1972; vol. 2: *Rezeption, Argumentation, Diskussion.* Freiburg i.Br., 1974.

Ritter, Joachim. "Moralität und Sittlichkeit: Zu Hegels Auseinandersetzung mit der kantischen Ethik" (first published 1966). In Ritter, *Metaphysik und Politik: Studien zu Aristoteles und Hegel,* pp. 281–309. Frankfurt a.M., 1969.

" 'Politik' and 'Ethik' in der praktischen Philosophie des Aristoteles" (first published 1967). In Ritter, *Metaphysik und Politik: Studien zu Aristoteles und Hegel,* pp. 106–32. Frankfurt a.M., 1969.

Rorty, Richard. "The World Well Lost." *Journal of Philosophy* 69 (1972), 649–65.

"Solidarity or Objectivity." In *Post-Analytical Philosophy,* edited by J. Rajchman and C. West, pp. 3–19. New York, 1986.

Ross, William David. *The Right and the Good.* Oxford, 1930.

Russell, Bertrand. *Introduction to Mathematical Philosophy.* London, 1919.

Ryle, Gilbert. *The Concept of Mind.* New York, 1971.

Sandel, Michael. *Liberalism and the Limits of Justice.* Cambridge, U.K. 1982.

Schaper, Eva. "Arguing Transcendentally." *Kant-Studien* 63 (1972), 100–16.

Schelling, Thomas. "Ethics, Law, and the Exercise of Self-Command." *Tanner Lectures on Human Values* 4 (1983), 43–79.

Schmucker, Joseph. *Die Ursprünge der Ethik Kants in seinen vorkritischen Schriften und Reflexionen.* Meisenheim, 1961.

Schneider, Hans Julius. "Der theoretische und der praktische Begründungsbegriff." In *Praktische Philosophie und konstruktive Wissenschaftstheorie,* edited by F. Kambartel, pp. 212–22. Frankfurt a.M., 1974.

Schöpf, Alfred. "Wille." In *Handbuch philosophischer Grundbegriffe,* vol. 3, edited by H. Krings, H. M. Baumgartner, and C. Wild, pp. 1702–22. Munich, 1973–4.

Schrader, George. "Autonomy, Heteronomy and Moral Imperatives." *Journal of Philosophy* 60 (1963), 65–77.

Schwemmer, Oswald. *Philosophie der Praxis: Versuch zur Grundlegung einer Lehre vom moralischen Argumentieren in Verbindung mit einer Interpretation der praktischen Philosophie Kants.* Frankfurt a.M., 1971.

"Grundlagen der normativen Ethik." In *Praktische Philosophie und konstruktive Wissenschaftstheorie,* edited by F. Kambartel, pp. 228–31. Frankfurt a.M., 1974.

"Letter to Kambartel." In *Praktische Philosophie und konstruktive Wissenschaftstheorie,* edited by F. Kambartel, pp. 228–31. Frankfurt a.M., 1974.

Searle, John R. *Speech Acts: An Essay in the Philosophy of Language.* Cambridge, U.K., 1969.

"Prima facie Obligations." In *Practical Reasoning,* edited by J. Raz, pp. 81–90. Oxford, 1978.

Sidgwick, Henry. *The Methods of Ethics* (first published 1874). London, 1901.

Simons, Eberhard. "Transzendentalphilosophie und Sprachpragmatik: Zur Methodik der Auseinandersetzung von Hermann Krings mit der transzendentalen Sprachpragmatik Karl-Otto Apels." In *Prinzip Freiheit,* edited by H.-M. Baumgartner, pp. 44–72. Freiburg, 1979.

Singer, Marcus. *Generalization in Ethics.* New York, 1971.

Snare, Frank. "Can a Moral Man Raise the Question: 'Should I Be Moral?'" *Canadian Journal of Philosophy* 4 (1975), 499–507.

Sobel, Howard J. "Interaction Problems of Utility Max-
    imizers." *Canadian Journal of Philosophy* 4 (1975), 677–88.
Sorabji, Richard. "Aristotle on the Role of Intellect in Virtue"
    (first published 1973–4). In *Essays on Aristotle's Ethics,* edited
    by A. Rorty, pp. 201–19. Berkeley, 1980.
Stephen, James F. *Liberty, Equality, Fraternity* (first published
    1873), edited by R. J. White. Cambridge, U.K. 1967.
Strawson, P. F. *Introduction to Logical Theory.* London, 1952.
Stroud, Barry. "Inference, Belief, and Understanding." *Mind* 88
    (1979), 179–96.
Taylor, Paul. "On Taking the Moral Point of View." *Midwest
    Studies in Philosophy* 3 (1978), 35–61.
Theunissen, Michael. *Sein und Schein: Die kritische Funktion der
    Hegel'schen Logik.* Frankfurt a.M., 1978.
Thomson, James, and Judith Thomson. "How Not to Derive
    'Ought' from 'Is' " (first published 1964). In *The Is–Ought
    Question,* edited by W. D. Hudson, pp. 163–7. London,
    1969.
Thomson, Judith. *Acts and Other Events.* Ithaca, 1977.
Thornton, J. C. "Can the Moral Point of View Be Justified?"
    Australasian Journal of Philosophy 42 (1964), 22–34.
Toulmin, Stephen. *An Examination of the Place of Reason in Ethics.*
    Cambridge, U.K., 1950.
Tugendhat, Ernst. "Drei Vorlesungen über Probleme der Eth-
    ik." In Tugendhat, *Probleme der Ethik,* pp. 57–131. Stutt-
    gart, 1984.
    "Retraktationen." In Tugendhat, *Probleme der Ethik,* pp. 132–
    76. Stuttgart, 1984.
Veatch, Henry B. "The Rational Justification of Moral Princi-
    ples: Can There Be Such a Thing?" *Review of Metaphysics* 29
    (1975–6), 217–38.
Vogel, C. J. de. "Quelques remarques à propos du premier
    chapitre de l'EN." In *Autour d'Aristote,* edited by S. Man-
    sion. Louvain and Paris, 1955.
Wadia, P. S. " 'Why Should I Be Moral' " *Australasian Journal of
    Philosophy* 42 (1964), 216–26.
Walhout, Donald. "Why Should I Be Moral? A Reconsidera-
    tion." *Review of Metaphysics* 12 (1959), 570–88.
Walker, Ralph. *Kant.* London, 1978.
Walzer, Michael. *Spheres of Justice.* Oxford, 1983.
Warnock, G. J. "Review of Grice." *Philosophical Quarterly* 18
    (1968), 374–5.
    The Object of Morality. London, 1972.

Watt, A. J. "Transcendental Arguments and Moral Principles." *Philosophical Quarterly* 25 (1975), 40–57.

Welker, Michael. *Der Vorgang Autonomie: Philosophische Beiträge zur Einsicht in theologischer Rezeption und Kritik.* Neukirchen, 1975.

Wellman, Carl. *A Theory of Rights: Persons under Laws, Institutions and Morals.* Totowa, N.J., 1985.

Wertheim, Peter. "Morality and Advantage." *Australasian Journal of Philosophy* 42 (1964), 375–87.

Whewell, William. *The Elements of Morality, Including Polity.* London, 1845.

White, Stephen. "On the Normative Structure of Action: Gewirth and Habermas." *Review of Politics* 44 (1982), 282–301.

Wiedmann, F., and Biller, G. "Klugheit." In *Historisches Wörterbuch der Philosophie,* vol. 4, edited by J. Ritter and K. Gründer, columns 857–63. Darmstadt, 1976.

Wiggins, David: "Deliberation and Practical Reason" (first published 1975–6). In *Essays on Aristotle's Ethics,* edited by A. Rorty, pp. 221–40. Berkeley, 1980.

Wildt, Andreas. *Autonomie und Anerkennung: Hegels Moralitätskritik im Lichte seiner Fichte-Rezeption.* Stuttgart, 1982.

Wilkes, Kathleen V. "The Good Man and the Good for Man in Aristotle's Ethics." *Mind* 87 (1978), 553–71.

Williams, Bernard. "Internal and External Reasons" (first published 1980). In Williams, *Moral Luck,* pp. 101–13. Cambridge, U.K., 1981.

Ethics and the Limits of Philosophy. Cambridge, Mass., 1985.

Winch, Peter. *The Idea of a Social Science and Its Relation to Philosophy.* London, 1958.

Wolf, Ursula. *Das Problem des moralischen Sollens.* Berlin, 1984.

Wolff, Robert Paul. *In Defense of Anarchism.* New York, 1970.

The Autonomy of Reason: A Commentary on Kant's Groundwork of the Metaphysic of Morals. New York, 1973.

Wright, Georg Henrik von. *Norm and Action.* London, 1963.

The Varieties of Goodness. London, 1963.

Zwingelberg, H. *Kants Ethik und das Problem der Einheit von Freiheit und Gesetz.* Bonn, 1969.

Index of names

Index of subjects